Edmond Rostand's

Cyrano
de Bergerac

Edmond Rostand's

Cyrano
de Bergerac

English Version by Charles Marowitz

Great Translations for Actors Series

SK
A Smith and Kraus Book

A Smith and Kraus Book
One Main Street PO Box 127 Lyme, NH 03768

First Edition: February 1995
10 9 8 7 6 5 4 3 2 1

Library of Congress Cataloging-in-Publication Data
Rostand, Edmond, 1868-1918.
        [Cyrano de Bergerac. English]
        Edmond Rostand's Cyrano de Bergerac / translated by Charles Marowitz. -- 1st ed.
                p. cm. -- (Great translations for actors series)
                ISBN 1-880399-68-7 : $11.95

        1. Cyrano de Bergerac, 1619-1655--Drama. 2. Authors, French--17th cen
        tury--Drama. 3. France--History--17th century--Drama. 4. France--History--17th cen
        tury--Drama. [1. Cyrano de Bergerac, 1619-1655--Drama. 2. Authors, French--17th
        century--Drama.] I. Marowitz, Charles. II. Title. III. Title: Cyrano de Bergerac.
        IV. Series.

        PQ2635.07C913   1994   94-41837
        842'.8--dc20   CIP
                                                        AC

Contents

Charles Marowitz has over two dozen books to his credit, the most recent being *Recycling Shakespeare*, a collection of Shakespearean criticism. Previous to that, a souvenir of his London years, *Burnt Bridges* was published in the UK.

He has made three adaptations from the French; two of these Ionesco's *Makbett* and Arrabal's *And They Put Handcuffs on the Flowers* were published by Grove Press. His translations and adaptations of plays by Ibsen and Strindberg were published under the title *Sex Wars* and his free adaptation of Oscar Wilde's *The Critic As Artist* was published both in the UK and Germany.

His collection *Potboilers* consists of three black comedies including the play *Sherlock's Last Case* which was presented on Broadway in 1987 starring Frank Langella. His plays *Wilde West*, *Disciples* and *Clever Dick* are published by Dramatists Play Service.

In the mid-sixties, Marowitz began producing a series of radical, free-styled adaptations of Shakespeare, the first of which, *The Marowitz Hamlet*, was premiered by the Royal Shakespeare Company and was performed subsequently at the Akademie der Kunste in Berlin. That and six other Shakespearean treatments were published under the title, *The Marowitz Shakespeare* and are performed with regularity world-wide. His book on acting, *The Act of Being* is a popular text book with universities in England and the USA. His play-reviews from the 60s and 70s are in the Methuen collection, *Confession of a Counterfeit Critic*.

He has been the lead critic for the *LA Herald Examiner* in California and is currently the West Coast Theater Critic for *Theater Week Magazine* in New York.

PUBLISHER'S PREFACE

Those who wish to read the great works of a foreign literature must learn the language or depend on the kindness of translators; and every translation must try to recover both the letter and the spirit of the original. Translators must know two languages so intimately that it's more than a metaphor to call it "by heart." They must also have some writer's instinct to understand how best to recreate the essence of the original work, from the most seemingly spontaneous elements of its style to the most profound of its ideas.

The sense of a work is more easily translated than its particular sound, and we may apprehend the narrative or the ideas of the original even as we complain that it all sounds "like a translation." The hardest task of the translator is to determine what in the very language of a piece makes it sound like Chaucer, or Dickens, or Joyce, and then discover how those qualities can be recapitulated in a different language. It don't mean a thing, alas, if it ain't got that swing.

There are singular problems in attempting to translate works for the theater. Special care must be taken to make the work sound right—and Molière does not sound like Racine. Care must also be taken, however, to make the lines easy for actors to speak: a play is a live experience in which a reality is conjured that must include the unforced participation of actors and audiences. Care must also be taken to preserve the particular flavor of the individual characters: old men, for example, don't have the same vocabularies and rhythms as young girls. In addition, the language of the translation should give us something of the time and the place of the original play.

Smith and Kraus aspires to bring great plays from other countries and cultures into new, vital, and eminently actable American translations. For too long, high school and college productions of Ibsen or Chekhov, for example, have put a distorting screen of British sensibility between the great playwrights, on the one side, and our actors and audiences on the other, because of British translations. It is absurd, but unhappily not uncommon, for young American actors playing servants and lower class types to struggle with Cockney accents in Norwegian or Russian plays.

"Translations for actors": we here at Smith & Kraus take our motto very seriously. We promise you that the translations we bring you will be so faithful, fresh, and eloquent you will want to read the plays out loud. Crafted especially for production, they will help you plunge deep inside the original work. They will never block your way.

Introduction

Like most adolescents of my period, I fell in love with 'Cyrano de Bergerac' around the time I started high school. The love affair was consummated when the Stanley Kramer film starring Jose Ferrer appeared making concrete the fanciful longings stirred by the text.

When I reached the age of discretion, I thought back to 'Cyrano' as one would a teenage romance which, though largely an infatuation, still left indelible marks. As one became aware of the riches of Shakespeare and Marlowe, Dryden and Webster, Edmond Rostand's talent became, in retrospect, brittle, even negligible. Later on however, after one had become somewhat weighed down with the heavyweight classics, one returned with a renewed appreciation for the simpler pleasures of works like 'Cyrano'. In one's maturity, it became clear that art, like food, had different densities— and sometimes a burger and a milkshake were preferable to a four course meal and provided a gastronomic high of an entirely different order.

It is Edmond Rostand's curse that one always begins by qualifying his talent and apologizing for his work—as if liking Rostand was tantamount to culturally slumming. This is an impulse that never arises when watching his play but seems to be unavoidable in critical evaluations. Therefore, let me say at the outset that, just as Herrick and Campion need suffer no sense of inferiority when compared to Shakespeare and Marlowe, so there is no need for us to justify our liking for Rostand. In fact, to put things into proper perspective, 'Cyrano de Bergerac' is a far sturdier piece of craftsmanship than 'Pericles' or 'The Siege at Rhodes,' confirmed by the fact that it has not been out of the modern repertoire since its first production in 1897.

At a time when the universal surge was towards naturalism (specifically, in France, Andre Antoine, *Theatre Libre* and the legatees of Zola), Rostand chose to aggrandize artifice and elevate whimsy. Even the non-naturalistic esthetics of Maeterlinck left him cold. His was a theatre of the heart pitted against the rigours of the mind eschewing the fashionable doctrine which revered the social sciences. He did not so much swim against the tide as straddle a branch above it and watch it flow in other directions. There is something gratifying about that kind of artistic aloofness in an age, like our own, when everyone else was metaphorically wearing pins and subscribing to one 'school' or another.

Immersing oneself in Rostand, I was constantly reminded of Thomas Rowe, the 18th century playwright who apart from being a hopeless Shakespeare-groupie was also one of his first editors and a successful playwright in his own right. Rowe was grossly derivative of Shakespeare and virtually nothing he wrote had the distinction or quality of his mentor, but he did produce a rapid, functional, eminently speakable kind of dramatic verse which made works such as 'The Fair Penitent' and 'Jane Shore' play with verve and efficacy. To discuss Rostand in the same breath as Molière or Corneille, Racine or Marivaux is to relegate him to some lower echelon of creativity. But just as there are certain kinds of theatrical effects in which Rowe succeeds far better than Shakespeare, so there is a certain resilient romanticism in Rostand which one can find in almost no other French playwright—including Victor Hugo and Dumas *fils* whose progeny he would appear to be. It is the sinuous and ebullient verse of a 'minor' poet which, because of his sense of dramaturgy and intellectual independence, occasionally produces 'major' effects.

The last thing Rostand is interested in is the well made play. He, like his rambunctious hero, instinctively recoils from anything as prefabricated as that. As AGH Spier wrote in the twenties, Rostand's work "is divided into three parts which we might call the statement of the ideal, the test and the confirmation" and 'Cyrano' clearly exemplifies this pattern. There are whole chunks of the play which, evaluated according to established play-writing techniques, could be deleted because they do not help the plot proceed to that point of resolution to which traditional plays usually tend. But if one did delete them, one would be losing the pearls that give the crown its glitter. Apply the traditional yardstick to a work like 'The Importance of Being Earnest' and you could reach the same conclusion—but the virtues of that play, as with 'Cyrano,' are in the amplifications, the digressions, the, if you like, irrelevancies. Sometimes it is texture which determines the quality of content and, in such cases, one must revere the peculiarities of a text as one does the peculiar characteristsics of an individual who, outsize and unorthadox, is, for those very reasons, more fascinating.

The play is predicated on the irresistible lie that wit, talent and personal panache cannot only compensate a man for physical ugliness but also enable him to triumph over competition which is patently more attractive. It is the pipe dream of every acne-ridden schoolboy and tubby, balding Romeo who watches the good-looking jock waltz off with the most desirable campus beauties. It elevates the idea of esthetic worth to a height as fanciful as it is unreal. Perhaps that is why the play is juvenile in the very best sense of that word and, for a century, has been so highly appreciated by very young people. Its own intrinsic romanticism speaks persuasively to people who have not yet lost their sense of romance. It is redolent of the fairy tales on which young persons have been weaned. It is a literary extrapolation of 'Beauty and the Beast,' 'The Ugly Duckling' and all those other fables where unprepossessing heroes improbably win the hands of fairy princesses. In other words, it nourishes the fantasy quotient in men and women which, unfortunately, attenutates as they grow older and wiser—i.e. mundane and cynical. It is, if you like, 'children's theatre' on the very highest level—because, mythic roots notwithstanding, its branches yield the ripe fruit of culture and poetry. The hero of 'Cyrano de Bergerac' is not the eponymous hero based on the real adventurer and poet of the mid 17th century but Poetry itself; the poetic notion of life as opposed to its prosaic counterpart; fancy as opposed to fact; dream-life as oppposed to real-life. Cyrano's adventure, both in the play and in his own life, exemplified the kind of action and endeavor which is no longer available to us in our own lives—except through emulation of make-believe heroes in books, plays and films. That is why we continually come back to Cyrano. He represents the freedom, independence, nonchalance and impetuosity which we barter away in order to become responsible citizens—qualities which we never forgive the adult world from taking from us.

Cyrano de Bergerac, sometimes Hercule de Bergerac, often referred to as Savinien de Cyrano de Bergerac, was born in Paris in 1619 and brought up by a country priest in a small private school. It was there that he first met his friend Henri Lebret; a friendship that was to last a lifetime. When a certain strain appeared in the relations between teacher and pupil, Cyrano was sent back to Paris to the *College de Beauvais,* where he was put under the charge of an even more disagreeable disciplinarian called Grangier who was later cruelly characterized by the author in a comedy entitled 'Le Pedant Jouè.'

Once in the capitol, Cyrano conspicuously sowed his wild oats, so much so that his father threatened to disown him. Lebret, Horatio to Cyrano's Hamlet, effected a reconciliation of sorts and persuaded his friend to join him in the *gardes nobles* under the command of the very same Captain Carbon de Castel Jaloux who inhabits Rostand's play. It was here that Cyrano was nicknamed *le demon de bravoure* and lived up to that name with several foolhardy acts of bravery. These became even more spectacular when he went to fight for his King in Flanders against the Spanish. He was wounded at Mouzaon and at Arras then mustered out of the service, which he didn't seem to mind for, not having an influential patron, he felt he never achieved the rank he deserved. From then on, he immersed himself almost entirely in the pursuit of science and literature, becoming an enthusiastic disciple of Epicurian philosophy.

Between 1648 and 1653, he lived an itinerant life and then entered the service of the Duc d'Arpajon to whom he dedicated several of the books written during this period, the most successful of which was the aforementioned 'Le Pedant Joue.' Like Alfred Jarry whom he spiritually resembles, his most significant early work was inspired by profound contempt for a repellent authority figure. (Clearly there was an abundance of Pere Ubu's in the French educational system of the 17th century as there were two centuries later.) His play 'The Death of Agrippine' which appeared in 1654 was also dedicated to his patron, but its atheism caused such a violent reaction, the Duke tried to distance himself from both the work and its author. After making innumerable, highly-placed enemies, he was wounded by a piece of timber dropped from an upper story of the Duke's residence just as he was entering the grounds. The Duke, out of concern (or possibly to rid himself of his troublesome charge), suggested it might be best for Cyrano to recuperate in the country which, rankling at his patron's callousness, he did. He spent fourteen months with a royal counsel who lovingly looked after him and created the conditions under which Cyrano was able to complete his last works, most notably 'Voyage To The Moon' and 'The History of the Republic of the Sun.'

It was during this period of enforced convalesence that attempts were made to convert Cyrano to Catholicism. Lebret claimed the efforts were successful but since Cyrano left this gaggle of religious zealots five days before his death, it is more likely that he died an atheist—at the home of his cousin, Pierre de Cyrano in September 1655.

The size of Cyrano's nose was also a matter of historical fact—and like his namesake in Rostand's play, he gloried in it. From firsthand accounts of those who have seen portraits of the soldier-poet, it was "monumental." The incident in which he comes to Ligniere's defense when his friend is threatened by vengeful aristocrats, is also based on fact as was his victory over incredible odds at the *Porte de Nesle*. We do not know precisely the cause of his quarrel with the actor Montfleury, but he *did* ban him from the stage for a month and when the actor attempted to break the ban, Cyrano *did* beard him in his own den to the consternation of a vociferous audience, many of whom were more predisposed to Montfleury than to Cyrano.

His fanciful, pseudo-scientific writings still exist in French; the most fascinating being his imaginary voyages to the moon and the sun which pre-date Swift's 'Gulliver Travels' and are strongly reminiscent of it. It is inconceivable that Jules Vernes did not come under Cyrano's influence. His works ran to several editions for three centuries after his death.

Is this the same Cyrano that Rostand has rendered? Not in every particular. Cyrano himself was a rather scurrilous and aggressive antagonist who took great joy in cruelly demolishing his enemies—and not always with great style or elegance. But in the life of Cyrano there is an 'against the grain' quality which clearly appealed to the playwright who himself ran counter to the theatrical fashion of his day and who may have used the historical character as a ramrod to batter social and esthetic tendencies that he despised. But there is no denying the fact that because there is a real, decipherable, flesh-and-blood personage behind Rostand's character, the play is nourished by very much more than poetic fancy. Behind its heroics and ornamentation, there is a rock-solid foundation which, being part of 17th century French history, gives it solidity as turn-of-the-century French drama.

A WORD ABOUT TRANSLATION IN GENERAL AND THIS ONE IN PARTICULAR.

Almost every word-cluster contains several connotations, many of them suggesting idiomatic usages or contemporary turns-of-phrase which did not exist at the time the work was first created. A phrase means not only what it says but what it connotes in action, inference and implication. By the same token, a stage direction may often convey the exact meaning imparted to a speech.

Sometimes a negative construction serves to convey what, in the original, was a declarative sentence and vice verse. Sometimes a contiguous idea, implied but not stated, asks to take the place of the line which suggested it. Sometimes a thought inspired by something stated suggests itself to ramify an original statement. What is being translated in these instances is not so much language as ambiance, subtext rather than text, incipient rather than manifest meaning, but in all cases, thoughts and ideas brought into being by the author's original text.

One talks constantly about the 'spirit' as opposed to the 'letter' of a text but what is not acknowledged is that the capture of 'spirit' must often be at the *expense* of the 'letter' and that sometimes it is the author's literal meaning which impedes the conveyance of its 'spirit' from one language to another, one historical period to another.

Some of the words in this version cannot be traced back directly to Rostand—although all of them were instigated by ideas, situations, inferences and hints contained in his original work. An 'original translation,' if it is not to be a misnomer, must *originate* modes of expression triggered by the original and not always interchangeable with its literal meaning. Some of the worst translations I know are faithful to works which, given the changed linguistic and historic contexts, would never dream of being faithful to themselves.

I am aware that this opens up a yawning chasm into which freewheeling translators are consigned by participle-pinching purists. The only defense can be the work itself, as no hard and fast rules can be formulated which give a translator specific parameters within which to be 'creative' at the expense of an author's original work. The essential question is *what* is being translated? If one accepts that a play is its ambiguities and associations as well as its language, it widens the translator's brief and increases his areas of responsibility.

The liberties taken with the blank verse are not unlike those taken by Shakespeare in his later period. Where there is an iambic foot missing, it usually means a pause is intended. Broken bits of pentameter divided between several characters indicate a rapid speech-pattern. When the dramatic situation becomes jagged or uneven, the verse usually follows suit. Where a trochee seemed serviceable, it replaced an iamb in what was essentially a stretch of iambic pentameter. The only scene entirely in prose is the one in which Cyrano pretends to be a space traveller to forestall De Guiche's interruption of Roxane and Christian's nuptials. This scene is so off-the-wall and distinct from everything else around it, it seemed to me to justify the excursion into prose. It is also, incidentally, the one scene that brings us closest to the historical Cyrano's obsession with science fiction. It follows from all the foregoing that the reason I have called this an 'English Version' rather than a translation, is because I have deliberately taken a personalized rather than punctilious approach in rendering the material.

This version was made with actors uppermost in mind and stage verse, unlike literary poetry, needs immediately to convey intent and not merely inspire meditation. Although 'Cyrano' has been criticized for being a play dominated by only one fully realized character, the fact is it contains dozens of perfectly-rounded cameo roles from Ragueneau, the poetic pastry chef who loses his faithless wife to a macho musketeer, to The Duenna whose dry wit rescues her from being an anonymous stock-character shadowing Roxane. Le Bret, Cyrano's Horatio, is also fully conceptualized and amply delineated as is Captain Carbon Castel-Jaloux and even the—*en passant*—Montfleury. The last three, like Cyrano himself, were based on actual historical characters but that is not what accounts for their definition. It is the fact that Rostand was too good a playwright simply to provide padding and so virtually every secondary character, like a skillful pencil-sketch, has the semblance of life and a style peculiar to him or herself.

Much of the romantic extravagance of Cyrano is only possible today if played tongue-in-cheek—but it is worth pointing out, a great deal of it was tongue-in-cheek to begin with. It is the subtle humor lodged in the very marrow of Rostand's play which has enabled it to thrive for almost a hundred years. Its shuttling between the grandiose and the self-deprecatory is what gives it its modernistic tone. Despite volleys of high rhetoric and windy pomposity, it really does not take itself very seriously at all. In this, it is winningly postmodernist and reminds us of stand-up comics and TV situation comedy which are similarly two-faced and ironic.

Roxane, a sequestered, church-going innocent, constantly accompanied by a strict chaperone, nevertheless falls impetuously in love at first sight, risks life and limb to visit her lover at the front and is as charmingly zany as the Pin-Up girl of the Gascon Cadets as she is demure with Christian and duplicitious with De Guiche. Rostand toys with her and winks at us, urging us to play along with him. It is to his credit as a playwright that when, in the final scene, he wishes this artificial creature to be touching and poignant, he manages to make us forget how loopy she had been only moments before.

Christian is an inarticulate airhead who crasssly wants to take advantage of his beloved after Cyrano has provided the poetic foreplay—and although he is almost goofy in the balcony scenes, we feel a pang when we learn of his death. In this way, a sure footed dramatist can move from puerility to pathos, from playful artificiality to compelling truth—sometimes within moments of the same scene. These are skilful dramaturgical transitions and even Shakespeare isn't always as ambidextrous as Rostand in bringing them off.

De Guiche is nothing like the villain of traditional melodrama which flourished across the English Channel at around the same time this play premiered. He is elevated by being genuinely enamored of Roxane and, despite his foppishness, when it comes to the crunch, he reveals himself to be as virile and courageous as any of the Gascons under his command. Cyrano needs a villainous foil and, in the middle acts, De Guiche, hard-hearted and vindictive, serves the purpose, but his blue blood saves him from ever becoming a bloody-minded 'heavy' in the tradition of Iago or Iachimo. In the soft-centered world devised by Rostand, even the blackguards have an air of comic opera about them and the entire text, a striking similarity to a libretto.

As for Cyrano himself, the richness of the character is that he can be given whatever emphasis an actor chooses and so his longevity in the dramatic repertoire is guaranteed. He is outlandish and extravagant but also timid and insecure; an efficacious poet and yet a frustrated lover; a canny strategist as well as an impulsive daredevil; an ostentatious showman but also a man fearful of exposing himself to public scrutiny. It is as much the times as the man that engenders the play's romance. This is a period when to be articulate is as impressive as being valorous; finding precisely the right phrase to skewer one's enemy as important as defeating him in a duel. Style is Cyrano's secret weapon; it is also the secret of Rostand's play.

—*Charles Marowitz*

Cyrano
de Bergerac

Main Characters

Cyrano de Bergerac
Christian de Neuvillette
Comte de Guiche
Ragueneau
Le Bret
Carbon Castel-Jaloux
The Cadets
Ligniere
Vicomte de Valvert
Three Marquis
Montfleury

Additional Characters

Bellerose
Jodelet
Cuigy
Brissaille
A Kibitzer
Musketeer With Moustache
A Spaniard
A Cavalier
A Porter
A Tradesman
Tradesman's Son
A Doorkeeper
Pickpocket
Spectators
A Sentry
Bertrandou, a fifer
A Capuchin
Two Musicians
Pastrycooks
Poets

Pages
Roxane
The Duenna
Lise
The Orange Girl
Mother Marguerite
Sister Martha
Sister Claire
An Actress
A Soubrette
A Flower Girl
Nuns
Intellectual Ladies
Theatre-Crowd, Citizens,
    Musketeers, Actors, Lackeys,
    Musicians,
Children, Spanish Soldiers,
    Spectators, Intellectuals,
    Academicians.

Cyrano de Bergerac

Act I

The year, 1640; the place, the Hall of the Hotel de Bourgogne. Originally a tennis court but now fitted up and decorated for theatrical performances.

Although a long rectangle, we are viewing the Hall diagonally. On one side, we see the back of the stage which starts at the First Entrance, Stage Right, and runs to the last entrance, Stage Left. There, it intersects with the stage proper which can be glimpsed obliquely.

There are benches on the stage that run the length of the wings. The curtain is a hanging piece of tapestry divided in the middle. Above Harlequin's cloak are the Royal Arms. A broad set of stairs lead from the stage to the floor of the Hall; places for musicians are on either side. The footlights are a row of lit candles. Along the side, two galleries, one above the other. In the upper gallery, a number of private boxes.

There are no seats on the parterre which is the actual stage of the theatre. Towards the back however, a few tiers of benches have been arranged. Under a staircase which leads to the upper gallery, there is a makeshift sideboard containing candelabra, vases of flowers, glasses, dishes with cake, bottles, etc.

In the center, beneath the tier of boxes, is the main entrance, a great door through which the audience will be admitted. On the portals of these doors as well as elsewhere around the Hall, there are playbills proclaiming the afternoon's performance: 'La Clorise.'

At Rise, the Hall is in half-light and empty. The chandeliers descend from above to the floor below, waiting to be illuminated. Gradually, the public begin to congregate; courtiers, tradesmen, lackeys, pages, thieves, pickpockets, etc. followed by the musicians and the more courtly members of the audience.

DOORKEEPER: *(following hard upon a* GENTLEMAN *who has just swept in)*
    Hey there, fifteen sou!
GENTLEMAN:
    I never pay.
DOORKEEPER:
    How come?
GENTLEMAN:
    Member of the Palace Guard.
DOORKEEPER: *(as a second man breezes past him)*
    Fifteen sou!
CAVALIER:
    I never pay.
DOORKEEPER:
    How come?
CAVALIER:
    Musketeer.

(The DOORKEEPER, *intimidated by their manner, moves off.)*

GENTLEMAN: *(to the* CAVALIER*)*
    The play begins at two. The house is empty;
    The stage bare. *(brandishing his foil)* Let's try
                some turns of our own.
    (They draw swords and make a few passes at each other.)
LACKEY: *(entering)*
                Pssst...Flanquin!
ANOTHER: *(already in)*
                Champagne?
1ST LACKEY: *(shuffling cards in one hand, dice in the other)*
                Cards! Dice! *(sits)*
                        Let's have a go.
2ND LACKEY: *(revealing his own cards and dice)*
    You're on.

1ST LACKEY: *(takes a sawn-off candle, lights it and sets it on the floor)*
I've nicked a bit of tallow from my master.
He'll never miss it.

GUARDSMAN: *(putting his arms around a flower girl who has just entered)*
                    Cherie. — It always pays
To get here early.

GENTLEMAN: *(receiving a hit)*
A hit!

2ND LACKEY:
Clubs.

GUARDSMAN: *(imploring)*
One little kiss.

FLOWER GIRL: *(drawing away)*
                    They'll see us.

GUARDSMAN: *(drawing her into dark corner)*
                    Not in here.

A MAN: *(sitting on the floor with a group of others, breaking out bread and
cheese)*
It's always nice to have little snack
Before the show.

TRADESMAN: *(with his young son in tow)*
                              Sit here, m'boy.

1ST LACKEY:
                                    Aces!

2ND MAN: *(producing a bottle of wine and sitting with others)*
Burgundy tastes best, I always say
When it's downed among Burgundians.

TRADESMAN: *(to his son)*
A fouler den of vice you'll never see,
(pointing with his cane at some drunks)
Drunkards…
(As the duellists part, one pushes him over.)
                    Brawlers…
(Tripping over the card-players.)
                              Gamblers! — N'er do-wells.

GUARDSMAN: *(behind him, still struggling with the flower girl)*
One little kiss.

TRADESMAN: *(drawing his son away)*
                    Good God! To think, in such
A place they play Corneille.

3

SON:

And Molière too.

PAGES: *(enter dancing a farandole and holding hands)*
Tra-la la la la la la la lere…

THE DOORMAN: *(admonishingly)*
Settle down; we don't want any trouble.

1ST PAGE: *(with mock dignity)*
What an idea? *(Then when DOORKEEPER turns away)*
Psst, you got the string?

2ND PAGE: *(displaying it)*
And the hook.

1ST PAGE:

Then up we go to the gallery
And see if we can *(mimes fishing)* catch ourselves some wigs.

PICKPOCKET: *(gathering his cohorts around him)*
Now listen close and mark the lesson well,
Since this is your first 'go' at lifting purses…

2ND PAGE: *(calling to other PAGES in the gallery)*
Pea-shooters, en garde?

3RD PAGE:

— All peas at the ready!

2ND PAGE:
Take aim, my fusileers, and fire at will!

(The PAGES from the galleries shower those below with peas. They look around but the PAGES have ducked out of sight.)

THE SON:
What's the play today?

TRADESMAN:
'La Clorise'

THE SON:
And who's it by?

TRADESMAN:

Balthazar Baro.
Brilliant. Just wait 'til you see it.
(kisses his thumb and index finger indicating 'exquisite' then takes his son by the arm and moves off)

PICKPOCKET: *(to his student-thieves, demonstrating with mime)*
Just snip the lace around those gorgeous sleeves.

4

A SPECTATOR: *(to his companion, pointing above)*
    That's where I sat on the first night of 'Le Cid'!
PICKPOCKET:
    Watches — out!
    (mimes snatching them)
                        then — in!
    (mimes slipping them down his sleeve).
                                then gracefully
    Move on. The main thing is — don't ever look back.
TRADESMAN: *(to his son)*
    The greatest actors of this or any day...
PICKPOCKET:
    Linens!

(Mimes opening the pocket on the right, drawing out the handkerchief and blithely pocketing it on the left.)

TRADESMAN:
    Montfleury —
ANOTHER SPECTATOR: *(in the upper gallery)*
                        Light the lights!
TRADESMAN: *(intoning the names of the great actors)*
    Bellerose, l'Epy, Beaupré, Jodelet!
A PAGE: *(in the parterre)*
                                Ah, refreshments!
ORANGE GIRL: *(appearing with her basket)*
    Oranges! Milk! Raspberry-squash! Lemonade —

(There is a great clatter at the door.)

A FALSETTO VOICE:
    Make way, you brutes!
1ST LACKEY: *(surprised)*
                                The Marquis? In the pit?

(A small group of Marquises enters.)

2ND LACKEY:
    Not for long. — They'll soon take their seats
    Upon the stage as they always do, you'll see.

1ST MARQUIS: *(scanning the half-empty Hall)*
    We enter just like everyone else. No fuss.
    No bother. No treading on toes. O, how we have
    Come down in the world!
    (encountering two regal friends)
                                    Cuigy! Brissaille!
    (They embrace ostentatiously.)
CUIGY:
    Ah, the ever-faithful 'devotees'
    — Always here before the lights are up.
1ST MARQUIS: *(uppity)*
    Be quiet! — You're always getting me into a state!
2ND MARQUIS: Shh! — The lights are going up!

(The CROWD applauds the arrival of the LAMPLIGHTER and 'oohs' and 'ahs' as he proceeds to light the candles. A certain number of spectators have already taken their places in the Gallery. LIGNIERE enters the main hall arm in arm with CHRISTIAN DE NEUVILLETTE. LIGNIERE, though dishevelled and dissipated still manages to look distinguished. CHRISTIAN, attractive and well-built, is elegantly attired but not really fashionable. He is clearly preoccupied and scans the boxes.)

CUIGY:

                                    Ligniere!

BRISSAILLE: *(smiling)*
    What, still sober at this time of day?
    Incredible! — Will wonders never cease? —
LIGNIERE: *(aside to CHRISTIAN)*
    May I do the honours?
    (CHRISTIAN nods agreement)
                        Baron de Neuvillete.

(They bow to one another. Meanwhile the crowd applauds enthusiastically as the lighted chandelier is hauled into position.)

CUIGY: *(to BRISSAILLE of CHRISTIAN)*
    Splendid looking fellow. Chiselled profile.
1ST MARQUIS: *(overhearing and disagreeing)*
    Fooh!
LIGNIERE: *(introducing them to CHRISTIAN)*

Messieurs de Cuigy... de Brissaille...

CHRISTIAN: *(bowing)*

Enchanté.

1ST MARQUIS: *(to the 2ND MARQUIS, re CHRISTIAN)*
Handsome, but not exactly 'a la mode'.

LIGNIERE: *(to CUIGY)*
Monsieur de Neuvillette has just arrived.

CHRISTIAN:

Indeed.

I've been in Paris just two weeks. Tomorrow
I join the Guards.

1ST MARQUIS: *(ogling as people take their seats in the boxes)*
Look, there's Madame Aubry.

(ostentatiously blows her a kiss)

ORANGE GIRL:
Oranges! Milk ! Squash!

(The Violins begin tuning up. CUIGY turns to CHRISTIAN and gesturing, says)

CUIGY:

Quite a crowd.

CHRISTIAN:
It's certainly filling up.

1ST MARQUIS:

It's nice to see
One's own on every side — the '*haut monde*'.

(They name the women as they enter the boxes dressed to the nines. There are exchanges of bows and smiles.)

2ND MARQUIS:
Madame de Guemenee...

CUIGY:

De Bois-Dauphin...

1ST MARQUIS:
Whom we adore...

BRISSAILLE:

Madame de Chavigny...

2ND MARQUIS:
Who toys with our affections.
LIGNIERE:
There's Corneille
Back from Rouen.
THE SON: *(to his father)*
And the Members of the Academy?
Are they here as well?
TRADESMAN:
Well, some of them.
There's Boudu-Boissat-Cureau-Porcheres-Arbaud.
Colomby-Bourzeys-Bourdon — deathless names.
Great men who'll never be forgotten.
1ST MARQUIS:
And look,
The Intelligentsia as well! You see,
There's Barthenoide, Urimedonte, Felixerie...
2ND MARQUIS:
O, the names alone just make me swoon.
You know them all, Marquis?
1ST MARQUIS: *(blasé)*
On first name terms.
LIGNIERE: *(taking CHRISTIAN aside)*
I came to offer services, my friend,
But alas, the lady's nowhere to be seen
So back to drink I go.
CHRISTIAN: *(entreating)*
No, just a moment.
She's always here. I've got to find a way
To meet her and to speak to her. The fact,
Is this: I'm sick with love for her. You know
The secrets of the town, the court, its ways.
Can't you find out her name?

(The conductor raps his bow for silence from the orchestra then gives a downbeat and the music starts up.)

ORANGE GIRL:
Macaroons!
Lemonade! Raspberry-squash!

(As the music plays softly behind, CHRISTIAN continues to implore LIGNIERE)

CHRISTIAN:

But then of course,
She may be one of those highbrow-ladies, rude
And full of wit. And then I would be lost.
How could I possibly talk to such a woman?
I have no words. No style. No polished ways.
I'm just a soldier, nothing more, and so, and so...
(pointing) That's where she sits, in that box, usually.

LIGNIERE: *(starts to leave)*

I'm off.

CHRISTIAN:

No, wait.

LIGNIERE:

I'm dying for a drink.
And there's a tavern fifty feet away.

ORANGE GIRL: *(passing by)*

Juice?

LIGNIERE: *(sourly)*

No!

ORANGE GIRL:

Milk?

LIGNIERE: *(making a face)*

Fhfft!

ORANGE GIRL:

Muscatel?

LIGNIERE:

Halt!

(He proffers a coin, she pours out his wine, he downs it in one gulp and turns to CHRISTIAN.)

You were saying.

(There is a hubbub at the door. Suddenly, a beaming, fat man dressed as a pastry cook enters and moves towards LIGNIERE.)

(aside to CHRISTIAN)

M'sieur Ragueneau.

RAGUENEAU:
　　Have you seen Cyrano? I've scoured the hall.
LIGNIERE: *(presenting him to* CHRISTIAN*)*
　　The pastry cook to poets and performers.
　　When artists starve, 'tis he that feeds the Muse.
RAGUENEAU: *(flattered)*
　　You do me too much honor.
LIGNIERE:
　　　　　　　　　　　　Manna from Heaven;
　　Eclairs from Ragueneau.
RAGUENEAU:
　　　　　　　　　　It's true enough
　　The artists gather round my stove —
LIGNIERE: *(aside)*
　　　　　　　　　　　　　　...on credit.
(flatteringly)
　　A poet as well!
RAGUENEAU: *(falsely modest)*
　　　　　　　　I dabble here and there.
LIGNIERE:
　　He *gorges* on verse.
RAGUENEAU:
　　　　　　　　　It's true that for an Ode,
　　I'd gladly trade a cream-filled cherry pie.
LIGNIERE:
　　And for a triolet?
RAGUENEAU:
　　　　　　　　A pair of rolls.
LIGNIERE: *(aside)*
　　Two days old. *(to* RAGUENEAU*)*
　　(flatteringly)　And a patron of the stage?
RAGUENEAU:
　　Can't get enough. A passionate devotee.
LIGNIERE:
　　He even barters tickets for his wares.
　　Your place today? How much did that cost you?
RAGUENEAU:
　　Four cream puffs and a week-old raspberry pie —
　　And cheap at the price, if you ask me. *(looks about)*
　　But Cyrano's not here.

LIGNIERE:
                    Why such surprise?
RAGUENEAU:
    Montfleury plays!
LIGNIERE:
                    Ah yes, that tub-of-lard
    Tonight assumes the role of Phedon. — So what?
RAGUENEAU:
    Don't you know? Don't say you haven't heard.
    M'sieur de Bergerac so hates the man
    He's forbidden Montfleury — for three full weeks —
    To appear upon the stage.
LIGNIERE: *(now on his fourth glass)*
                    The plot thickens.
RAGUENEAU:
    And Montfleury plays!
CUIGY: *(approaching with his coerie)*
                    And who's to stop him!?
RAGUENEAU:
    That's exactly what I've come to see.
1ST MARQUIS:
    Who is this Cyrano?
CUIGY:
                    The King of Cats,
    You might say. The longest, sharpest claws.
2ND MARQUIS:
    Is he well-born?
CUIGY:
                    Behaves as if he is.
    He's in the Guards.
    (Points to LE BRET who is wandering about looking for someone.)
                    There's his friend Le Bret.
    He can tell you more. — Hey, Le Bret!
    (LE BRET approaches)
    You're seeking Cyrano?
LE BRET: *(clearly worried)*
                    Indeed I am.
CUIGY:
    He's quite a chap, M'sieur de Bergerac.

LE BRET:
    The best friend and bravest soul alive.
RAGUENEAU:
    A poet!
CUIGY:
            Swordsman —
LE BRET:
                    Musician—
BRISSAILLE:
                            and Philosopher.
LIGNIERE:
    With a countenance, the likes of which
    No ordinary man would soon forget.
RAGUENEAU:
    I doubt that we shall see his portrait done
    In the solemn style of Philippe de Champagne.
    His bold extravagance is captured best
    By the garish brush of Jacques Callot,
    Who loved to paint those florid buccaneers.
    His hat, y'know, is wedged with three white plumes;
    His scabbard juts from underneath his cloak
    Just like the tail of an angry fighting-cock.
    Prouder than the proudest knights that graced
    The halls of Gascony, he bears beneath
    His wide chapeau, a nose — and *what* a nose
    It is, my lords! For as you watch it pass
    You think: 'Impossible, it *cannot* be.
    At any moment now he'll take it off.'
    But there it bulges like a camel's back,
    The very core of M'sieur de Bergerac.
LE BRET:
    Let him who would malign it best beware.
RAGUENEAU:
    His sword is like the Grim Reaper's sickle.
1ST MARQUIS: *(shrugging his shoulders)*
    He won't show up.
RAGUENEAU:
                  I say he will. What's more,
    I will wager your five francs against
    My Poulet a la Ragueneau.

Act I

1st Marquis: *(laughing)*

You're on!

(A soft murmur of admiration sweeps through the Hall as Roxane enters her box. She sits in front; her Duenna dressed in black, behind. Christian, busy with the Orange Girl, does not notice her.)

2nd Marquis: *(excitedly)*
Oh gentlemen, just cast your eyes on that.
Is she not ravishing?
1st Marquis:
A skin like peach.
A strawberry smile on tender crimson lips.
2nd Marquis:
Lips so cool they heat the blood and thus,
Make us all catch cold.
Christian:
O, there she is!
(Christian having just glimpsed Roxane takes Ligniere by the sleeve.)
Ligniere: *(cooly)*
Ah, the lady herself.
Christian:
What's her name?
Ligniere: *(sipping his Muscatel)*
Madeleine Robin, called Roxane… a wit,
Brainy, clever…
Christian: *(crestfallen)*
Oh dear.
Ligniere:
Unmarried.
Christian: *(revived)*
Ah!
Ligniere:
Good family, good stock, and cousin to Cyrano
Of whom we spoke a moment ago.

(A distinguished-looking gentleman wearing a Cordon Bleu around his neck has joined Roxane in her box and stands talking with her.)

CHRISTIAN:

                             And the man?

LIGNIERE:

    The wily Comte de Guiche; in love with her;
    But married to the niece of Richelieu—
    Herself the wife of old M'sieur de Valvert.
    A useful tool to de Guiche — you know what I mean.
    She's rejected his advances, — so far —
    But he's a dogged little chap, and she
    Alas, a child. — I've made a little song
    About his sordid little plot which has
    Not endeared me to the Comte, I fear.
    Would you like to hear the final chorus?

(He staggers to his feet, raises his glass aloft and is about to burst into song as CHRISTIAN *starts to leave.)*

CHRISTIAN:
    I'm off.
LIGNIERE: *(frozen in his musical tableau)*
        You're off? Off where?
CHRISTIAN:

                    To M'sieur de Valvert!

LIGNIERE:

    He's an expert swordsman. — He'll slice you in two.
    But wait, *(referring to* ROXANE *and* DE GUICHE*)*
        someone's got their eye on you.
CHRISTIAN: *(turning impetuously)*
    Roxane!…

(He stands spellbound, gazing at ROXANE. *As he does so,* THE PICKPOCKET *and his crew sensing a potential victim, gravitate in his direction.)*

LIGNIERE:

    Oh well, I must away. The wine shop beckons.
    *(*CHRISTIAN *still stands motionless.)*
    I'll sing it to you some other time. I know
    You're dying to hear it. — God, my throat is parched!

(He weaves out of the Hall in a zig-zag course. Meanwhile, LE BRET, having negotiated the Hall returns to RAGUENEAU.)

LE BRET:
    No sign of Cyrano.
RAGUENEAU: *(feeling he will show)*
                        Not yet… we'll see.
LE BRET:
    I only hope he hasn't seen the poster.
CROWD:
                                    The play! The play!
1ST MARQUIS: *(watches DE GUICHE exit ROXANE's box and cross to the parterre where he is met by a group of obsequious gentlemen, DE VALVERT among them)*
    (sarcastically of DE GUICHE)
    Quite an entourage.
2ND MARQUIS: *(dismissively)*
                        Still, — a Gascon!
1ST MARQUIS:
    But keen and cool and highly thought of too.
    It would be politic to pay our respects.

(They approach DE GUICHE.)

2ND MARQUIS:
    Gorgeous ribbons, Count. But what's the color?
    'Kiss me Quickly' or 'Robin Red-Breast'?

DE GUICHE:
                                    Neither.
    I call it 'Espagnole Malade'; that is,
    'The Sickly Spaniard'.

1ST MARQUIS:
                        Very aptly named
    For in Flanders under your command,
    The Spaniard's sure to sicken unto death.
DE GUICHE:
    Shall we sit upon the stage, Valvert?

CHRISTIAN: *(starting at the name)*
    Valvert! — That scheming pandar. — Where's my glove?
    I'll hurl it in his face.
    (Reaching for his glove, he finds the PICKPOCKET's hand already there.)
PICKPOCKET: *(caught)*
                O, bloody hell!
CHRISTIAN: *(holding on to the PICKPOCKET's wrist)*
    What's this? — I looked for a glove.
PICKPOCKET:
                      Instead,
    You find a hand? — Is it yours?
CHRISTIAN:
                          Mine? No.
PICKPOCKET:
    Then be so good as to return it to
    It's rightful owner.
CHRISTIAN: *(about to do so, realizes he's being toyed with, grabs it again)*
                Not so fast, M'sieur.
PICKPOCKET: *(bargaining)*
    Let me go! — I'll trade you information.
CHRISTIAN:
    What information?
PICKPOCKET:
                Ligniere? Your tipsy friend?
    As good as dead! A song of his offended
    One of the mighty. There'll be a hundred men
    Tonight will lay in wait for him. I know.
    I'm one of them.
CHRISTIAN:
             And on whose order, ey?
PICKPOCKET:
    Can't say.
CHRISTIAN: *(twisting his wrist)*
        Oh no?
PICKPOCKET: *(wincing)*
             Professional secret.
CHRISTIAN:
                  Then where?
PICKPOCKET:
    The Porte de Nesle. Just as he's heading home.

If you get to him in time, you'll save his life.
CHRISTIAN: *(freeing him)*
But where I am to find him?
PICKPOCKET:

Try the taverns:
The Golden Goblet, Pineapple Pete's, The Torches,
Sign Of The Broken-Buckle — Everywhere!
Leave a note of warning for your friend.
CHRISTIAN: *(starting out)*
A hundred men to one! The pack of cowards!
(fondly looking back to ROXANE)
Leave her? *(Looks angrily at VALVERT)* Leave him?
Damn! — I must rescue Liginiere!

(CHRISTIAN dashes out. DE GUICHE, THE VICOMTE, the MARQUISES have disappeared behind the curtains and taken their seats on the stage. The floor of the theatre is entirely filled with spectators as are the galleries and boxes. The house is overflowing.)

CROWD: *(clapping and chanting)*
The play! The play! Begin the play!
TRADESMAN:

My wig!

(It has been hoisted up to the gallery by a fishline held in the hands of one of the PAGES. The feat triggers great whoops of joy, cheers for the PAGES and unrestrained mocking laughter.)

TRADESMAN: *(shaking his fist at the gallery)*
You little scoundrels!

(The din of the spectators reaches a crescendo then subsides, then segues into complete silence as CARDINAL RICHELIEU resplendent in his robes, moves to take his seat in a box. Everyone is automatically hushed into a reverent silence.)

1ST PAGE: *(sotto voce)*
Damn it, now we've got to behave ourselves.

(THE CARDINAL stands in the box waiting for his seat. This soon becomes

evident and a chair is passed, hand to hand, from the parterre up to the Cardinals' box where a PAGE puts it in place. THE CARDINAL sits grandly; as his posterior hits the seat, a PAGE lets out a rude noise. THE CARDINAL withers him with a disdainful glance. The three traditional raps are heard off-stage. The Curtains open to reveal a Tableau. The background is of a pastoral scene painted in pastel shades. Four crystal chandeliers illuminate the stage. In the background, muted violins are heard.)

LE BRET: *(aside to RAGUENEAU)*
Will Montfleury appear?
RAGUENEAU: *(aside)*
His cue's been given.
LE BRET:
Cyrano's not here.
RAGUENEAU:
Then I've lost my bet.
LE BRET:
So much the better.

(A winsome shepherd's pipe is heard and an obese MONTFLEURY, rolls of fat overflowing his shepherd's costume and wearing a rose-laden hat, appears. He is playing a pastoral pipe festooned with ribbons. The CROWD applauds enthusiastically; some cry out 'Montfleury' and others 'Bravo'. The actor acknowledges the applause and begins to perform the role of Phedon.)

MONTFLEURY:
'How happy he who in sweet solitude
Escapes the pomp and power of the Court
And in the bosom of a leafy bower
Where balmy zephyrs cool his burning brow…'
VOICE:
Have I not banished you, wretch, for three whole weeks?

(A shock wave ripples through the House. Everyone turns to discover to whom the voice belongs. "What" "Where" "Who is it?")

LE BRET:
It's him.

CUIGY:

     Is it?

RAGUENEAU:

       Himself?

LE BRET:

         It's Cyrano.

VOICE:

  Whale-blubber! Quit the stage — at once!

(The CROWD is aghast at CYRANO's insolence and at the same time apprehensive.)

MONTFLEURY:

  I... I...

CYRANO:

     You hesitate, you dripping tub of lard?

  You dare to disobey?

VOICES IN THE CROWD:

  Quiet! — Let him play! — Go on, Montfleury —

  On with the play — Play on!

MONTFLEURY: *(in a tremulous voice)*

  "How happy he who in sweet solitude —

CYRANO:

  Must I lay a rod against your rump,

  You King of Clowns?

(A cane held in a firm hand juts out above the heads of the audience like a schoolteacher's birch about to mete out punishment.)

MONTFLEURY: *(In an even shakier voice)*

        '...who in sweet solitude

        Escapes the pomp and power of...'

(The cane is twirled threateningly, in the air.)

CYRANO:

  Out, I say!

  (Now in the center of floor, CYRANO suddenly appears. Standing erect upon a chair, his arms folded, his hat cocked, the moustache bristling, the formidable nose raised aloft.)

Or I shall really grow angry!

(At his menacing appearance, a palpable sensation ripples through the crowd.)

MONTFLEURY: *(imploring the Marquises)*
    Will you not protect a poor player, messieurs?
1ST MARQUIS:
    Play on!
2ND MARQUIS:
            Proceed!
CYRANO:
                    On your own head be it!
THE MARQUISES:
    Be still! Be quiet! Get off! Silence!
CYRANO:
    Unless these gentlemen remain aloof,
    I fear they'll find their lovely ribbons shredded —
    Among other things —
1ST MARQUIS: *(rising)*
                    This is too much!
CYRANO:
    Fly, goose! Or I'll turn your guts to garters,
    Pluck your feathers and trim your scraggly wings.
A VOICE: *(defensive)*
    See here…
CYRANO:
            Depart!
ANOTHER VOICE:
                Be still.
THIRD VOICE:
                    A moment —
CYRANO:
                            Still here?
    (dramatically rolling up his sleeves)
    Very good then I shall take the stage myself!
    'Enter Cyrano, with a naked blade, to cut
    Some slices off this gross Italian sausage.'
MONTFLEURY: *(lamely asserting his dignity)*
    An insult to Montfleury is an insult to the Muse.

CYRANO: *(with mock courtesy)*
> If She had the misfortune to make your acquaintance
> Then rest assured, the Muse would not forbear,
> Confronted with such corpulence, to aim
> A swift kick at your ample derriere.

CROWD:
> Montfleury, Montfleury! — On with the play.
> The play! the play! — 'La Clorise'
CYRANO: *(to those hecklers crowding around him)*
> Do not provoke my scabbard, gentle friends,
> Lest it stick its tongue into your hide.

(The circle grows larger around CYRANO.)

CYRANO: *(to Montfleury)*
> Begone, I say!

(As the crowd draws even closer around CYRANO, he suddenly turns on them, sword in hand. They instinctively recoil.)

(mock courteously, to the crowd)
> Did someone have something to say?
A VOICE FROM THE BACK: *(singing larkily)*
> "M'sieur Cyrano
> You tyrannize us well
> And consternate our peace.
> But though you dissent,
> You will not prevent
> Us from seeing 'La Clorise'
CROWD: *(bolstered by the song, all cry out in unison)*
> 'La Clorise'! 'La Clorise' ! 'La Clorise'!
CYRANO:
> One more repeat of that refrain and I'll
> Slay you all!
A CITIZEN: *(defiantly)*
> And are you Samson then?
CYRANO:
> Lend me a jawbone and you'll soon find out.

LADY IN A BOX:
 This is disgraceful!
A NOBLEMAN:
                    Scandalous!
TRADESMAN:
                         Infuriating!
MINCING PAGE:
                              …but quite amusing.

(This triggers a ferocious reaction from the CROWD *which proceeds to shout, shriek, moan, bay, bark and catcall.)*

CYRANO:
 Silence, you alley-cats.

(The din continues even wilder than before with the PAGES *imitating the sounds of cats, cockrels, ducks and apes. After a moment,* CYRANO *draws himself up to his full height, raises his hand and with a voice filled with invincible authority cries:)*

                    SILENCE, I say!
*(*CYRANO's *imperiousness has hushed the crowd.)*
I send this general challenge to you all!
Come, young worthies and all you brave gallants;
I'll take your names and issue each a number.
Who'd like to be the first man on the list?
You sir? — Or you perhaps? — Or shall it be you?
Whose blade is most impatient to be drawn?
To him I'll raise a monument in stone.
Let all who wish to die, now raise their hands!
(There is an uneasy silence.)
I see you're modest. You shrink away from death.
No volunteers? No heroes? Not a one?
(dropping his facetiousness)
Very well then; back to my affairs.
(Turns back to MONTFLEURY *who is trembling and looking very solitary on stage.)*
I wish this carbuncle to be removed
Or else, I fear *(putting his hand on his sword)*

22

I'll be obliged to lance it.
(CYRANO forsakes his chair and, as if strolling in his own parlor, seats himself in the midst of the circle which has formed around him.)
Here's a bit of stage-business for you,
Moon-faced Loon: I'll clap my hands three times
And on the third you shall — eclipse yourself.

(The crowd takes a wicked delight in the challenge. They turn stealthily to MONTFLEURY whose jitters are now even more pronounced.)

(Claps hands. Suddenly:)
                                              One!
MONTFLEURY:
    I…
VOICE FROM A BOX:
    Hang on.
CROWD MEMBER:
    Will he go?
2ND CROWD MEMBER:
    Or will he stay?
MONTFLEURY:
    Really, gentlemen, this is…
CYRANO: *(claps hands)*
    Two!
1ST MARQUIS: *(aside)*
    I'll wager ten to one against?
2ND MARQUIS: *(aside)*
    You're on.
MONTFLEURY:
    I have never in my entire career…
CYRANO: *(claps hands loudly)*
    Three!

(MONTFLEURY disappears — as if a trapdoor has swallowed him up. There is a wave of laughter, hoots, hisses and foot-stamping.)

MEMBERS OF THE CROWD:
    Come back, Coward!
CYRANO: *(luxuriating in a chair)*
                        Let him, if he dare.

(BELLEROSE, the Theatre Manager, tentatively comes forward. The audience, to whom he is a familiar face, mockingly applauds his cautious entrance on to the stage.)

BELLEROSE: *(with great formality)*
Most noble lords and respected ladies…
CROWD:
No pretty speeches. — Get off! — Jodelet!
Let's hear from Jodelet — the actor, Jodelet!

(JODELET, a favorite, is brought forward to address the audience. He speaks through his nose.)

JODELET:
Monsters, scoundrels, wifebeaters, layabouts and whores…

(The CROWD immediately warms to him.)

CROWD:
Hurrah. — Good man.— You tell 'em Jodelet. — Bravo!
JODELET: *(ironically)*
I crave your patience, gentles all! Alas,
Our fat tragedian whose girth is known
To one and all…
CROWD:
Coward. — Wheyface. — Worm. — Snail. —
JODELET:
      — craves your fair indulgence,
But is a trifle indisposed.
CROWD: Bring him back — 'La Clorise' — on with the play! —
THE SON: *(to CYRANO)*
But really m'sieur, I don't quite understand.
Why is it that you hate that Montfluery?
CYRANO: *(graciously, to the boy)*
Reasons have I two, dear boy, though each
Is strong enough to serve. First: as an actor,
He mouths the text like one who's eating porridge.
Or grunts and groans as if he were a porter
Carting verse that ought to soar like swallows
Up into the clouds. The second reason:

Well, that secret stays with me.
TRADESMAN:

But now
The play is closed. And 'La Clorise' by Baro
Denied to one and all.
CYRANO:
My dear old chap, since Baro is a bore
And turns out only drivel, I've done the arts
An inestimable service.
FEMALE INTELLECTUALS:
What cheek! — Our Baro? — a Bore? — Never! — The idea!
CYRANO: *(gallantly turning to the bluestockings in their box)*
Sweet ladies, shine your loveliness upon us,
Blossom like the flowers, and with grace,
Inspire us to poetry and song.
But as for criticism, — give it a rest.
BELLEROSE: *(highly irate)*
And what of all the takings? Do we simply
Give back all the money — just like that?
CYRANO: *(turning now to the stage)*
Bellerose, — the first to speak some sense!
I'll make no rents in Thespis honoured cloak.
(Throws him a purse.)
Take this! And let us hear no more about it.

(The crowd gasps with astonishment at CYRANO's beau geste.)

JODELET: *(Catches the purse and weighing it, passes it from one hand to the other. Then beamingly:)*
You have my leave, upon such generous terms,
To close us down whenever you may wish.
(The crowd boos vociferously.)
Boo on, with such returns, we'd even treat
A sell-out with disdain. Merci, monsieur.
BELLEROSE: *(officiously)*
Ladies and gentlemen, kindly clear the hall!
JODELET: *(mimicking Bellerose)*
Yes, kindly wheel your arses out the door.

*(The C*ROWD *begins to filter out as C*YRANO *looks on with satisfaction. But as the next scene begins, the exodus gradually stops. The women, their cloaks donned, malinger, and as they are drawn into the scene, again resume their seats.)*

LE BRET: *(admonishingly, to C*YRANO*)*
    You're mad!
A KIBITZER: *(rushing up to C*YRANO*)*
              But this is terrible, Montfleury!
    A star! His patron is the Duke de Candale.
    — Who's yours?
CYRANO:
    None.
A KIBITZER:
        None? You say none?
CYRANO: *(chiming in on the K*IBITZER*'s last word)*
                 None!
A KIBITZER:
    No nobleman to shield you with his name?
CYRANO: *(visibly annoyed)*
    I've said it twice, must I repeat again?
    The only patron I call mine hangs here
    Upon my belt.
A KIBITZER:
           But will you flee the city?
CYRANO:
    I may or I may not — who's to say?
A KIBITZER:
    Beware, the Duke de Candale has a very long arm.
CYRANO: *(drawing his sword)*
    Mine can be extended by three feet.
A KIBITZER:
    But surely man, you wouldn't dare…
CYRANO:
                There's nothing
    Sir, I "wouldn't dare." So go your ways,
    You are excused.
A KIBITZER:
          But I…

CYRANO:

You may depart!
Farewell.

(The KIBITZER still malingering, has his eyes fixed on CYRANO's nose which CYRANO now clocks.)

Are you staring at my nose?
A KIBITZER: *(flummoxed)*
Your nose—?
CYRANO: *(coming closer)*
Is there something wrong with it?
A KIBITZER: *(confused)*
Your grace mistakes…
CYRANO:

Is it loose perhaps,
And hanging like a trunk?
A KIBITZER:

I didn't mean to —
CYRANO:
Or crooked, like an owl's beak?
A KIBITZER:

I never —
CYRANO:
Do you espy a wart upon its furthest
Southern slope?
A KIBITZER:

Why no —
CYRANO:

Perhaps s a fly
Perambulating on its bridge? — Speak up!
A KIBITZER:
I didn't mean to look at all…
CYRANO:

Why not? —
Is it so repellent to the sight?
A KIBITZER:
I only —
CYRANO:

Its color so abominable?
Its shape, bizarre?

A KIBITZER:
                    No, not bizarre at all!
CYRANO:
    Then why this somewhat patronizing manner?
    Do you think it is a trifle large?
A KIBITZER: *(trying to contain his terror)*
    Not at all. It's really rather small.
    Miniscule, one might almost say.
CYRANO: *(slowly growing furious)*
    My nose, miniscule? You dare to call
    My nose miniscule!?
A KIBITZER: *(utterly flustered)*
                    I —, I —
CYRANO:
                    Enormous!
    My nose is *Gargantuan* — not flat
    Or snub or wee or pert or aquiline.
    An appendage that I wear with pride because
    A great nose is the emblem of a great man:
    Kindly, generous, brave and full of wit.
    All of which I am and you, poor toad,
    Will never be. Not in your wildest dreams!
    For that squat face which juts above your collar
    Proclaims a soul bereft of pride or sense,
    (emphasizing his points with slaps in his face)
    Of poetry or taste or joie-de-vivre.
    (takes him by the shoulders, turns him round and suiting the action to the word)
    The twin of that fat hulk which sags beneath
    Your spine and which my angry boot now pummels
    On its way!
    (A swift kick to the KIBITZER's posterior sends him flying.)
A KIBITZER: *(screeching off-stage)*
                    Help, help!
CYRANO:
                    So be advised:
    Those of you who find my countenance
    Amusing. — And for those among you who
    Are highly born, to those I say, take care:

My custom is to answer your disdain
More sharply still as well befits your station.
DE GUICHE: *(who, with the Marquises has descended from the stage)*
　　This braggart now grows tiresome.
VALVERT:
　　　　　　　　　　　　　　He blows
　　His own trumpet loudly.
DE GUICHE:
　　　　　　　　　　　　Is there no one
　　To put him in his place?
VALVERT:
　　　　　　　　　　　　　　　I'll take that chore
　　Upon myself, De Guiche. — Attend me well.
　　(VALVERT strides up to CYRANO and with an air of conscious affectation,
　　places himself directly in front of him.)
　　Your nose, you know, is — how shall I put it? —
　　Rather large.
CYRANO: *(gravely)*
　　　　　Rather…
VALVERT:
　　　　　　　　　Rather large!
　　(Suppresses a nervous laugh. Pause.)
CYRANO: *(imperturbable)*
　　Is that it?
VALVERT: *(slightly dismayed)*
　　　　　What's that?
CYRANO:
　　　　　　　　　Are you done?
VALVERT: *(uncertain)*
　　Yes, ha-ha — I think so.

　　(As he turns to go CYRANO bars his path.)

CYRANO:
　　　　　　　　But my dear fellow,
　　That will not do at all. There is so much
　　To say on such a topic, I can't believe
　　You'd throw away the chance. — You might begin
　　Par exemple, aggressively: "Were that
　　My nose, I'd have it surgically removed!"

Or Amiably: "How can you drink with such
A monstrous protuberance? Why I'd
Forego the mug and simply use a barrel!"
Descriptively: "Why it's a rock, a crag,
A promont'ry; an archipelago!"
Inquisitively: "I say, is it some kind of
Carrying-case for a trombone or a tuba?"
Courteously: " Do you adore the birds
So much that when the robins come to roost
You give them *that* to perch on?" Insolently:
"Be wary when you take a smoke, for sure,
They'll think your bloody chimney is on fire!"
Warily: "Don't tread on any marshes, —
The weight of it will sink you 'neath the ground."
Pensively: "Perhaps a large umbrella
Will stop the colors fading in the sun."
Pedantically: "Now Aristotle wrote
Of some enormous mythologic beast
'Hypocampelephantocamelos.'
(pointing to his nose)
Could this be the fiend he had in mind?"
Whimsically: "Now throw a tablecloth
Across the thing and all King Arthur's knights
Would have a place to sit." Eloquently:
"When it's blown, the typhoons rage and all
The hurricanoes roar." Rhetorically:
"When it bleeds, the Red Sea!" Practically:
"What a fitting shopfront it would make
For a parfumerie?" Or, Lyrically:
"The horn of Roland summ'ning Charlemagne
Was but a penny-whistle next to this!"
Respectfully: "O, may I lay a simple
Wreath beside the tow'ring monument?"
Rustically: "A nose, you say, pshaw!
It's a watermelon that's gone mad!"
Militarily: "Now, you take the right flank
And I, the left, and when I give the signal
We'll pound it till it drops!" Commercially:
"Raffle it off. It'd make a grand first prize!"
Or, as mighty Marlowe might have put it:

"Was this the nose that launched a thousand sniffs
And burned the topless towers of Illium?'
These, my friend, are things you might have said
Had you had some sprinklings of wit
To spice your tedious discourse. But alas,
You haven't got a grain of salt to spare.
You have no finesse and lack all letters.
(Sorry, you do have three: A - S - S!)
But even if you could somehow concoct
Some wounding jest before this company,
The chances are you'd never utter even
The first decibel of the first syllable,
For though I say these things about myself,
I never for a moment would endure
To have them said about me by another.

DE GUICHE: *(Trying to lead away the astonished VALVERT)*
    Vicomte, let's go.

VALVERT: *(All choked up)*
                    What arrogance; what airs!
    A clown — just look at him — no gloves — no lace —
    No buckles on his shoes — no handkerchief.

CYRANO:
    My adornments are not visible.
    I wear them all within *(hand to heart)*. Nor am I
    Caparisoned like a circus horse —
    Or stuffed with feathers like a popinjay.
    But you'll look in vain to find an insult
    That I have not with valor washed away.
    You'll find no ling'ring bile within my conscience;
    No honor frayed — no scruples cast aside.
    I glisten with bright emeralds unseen,
    My white plumes of freedom all embossed
    With my good name. — No, not a stalkinghorse,
    But a soul in shining armor, arrayed
    With deeds, not decorations. Twirling my wit
    Like moustachioes that go before me
    A deadly pair of swinging scimitars.
    A nerve of steel that throbs within my scabbard
    And, upon the clattering cobblestones,
    The echo of my bold, unvarnished truths

Reverberating like an Angelus.
VALVERT:
    However…
CYRANO: *(deprecatingly)*
           I haven't any gloves, alas.
    I did have one — the last of one old pair,
    But lost it rather carelessly I fear.
    A varlet dropped an insult I found base,
    And I'm afraid, I left it in his face.
VALVERT:
    Dolt! Knave! Wastrel! Booby! Clod!
CYRANO: *(assuming VALVERT has just introduced himself, CYRANO doffs his hat and does the same)*
    And I, Cyrano-Savinien-Hercule De Bergerac.
VALVERT: *(incensed)*
    Buffoon! Jackanape!
CYRANO: *(suddenly shrieks out loud as if with pain)*
           Aghhh!
VALVERT:
           Now what?
CYRANO: *(grimacing with false pain)*
    These horrid cramps will be the death of me.
    I've left it too long idle.
VALVERT:
           What's he saying?
CYRANO: *(now grim)*
    My sword has gone to sleep.
VALVERT: *(drawing his own sword)*
           I see. Well then,
    I'll rouse it soon enough.
CYRANO: *(meticulously)*
           I solemnly vow
    To transport you exquisitely into
    The Other World.
VALVERT:
           Vain, poetic braggart!
CYRANO:
    Indeed a poet, and to demonstrate
    My skill will, as I flay you, improvise
    A ballade, extempore.

VALVERT:

A ballade?

CYRANO: *(pedantically)*
Which, you may or may not know, consists
Of three eight-lined stanzas and refrain
Containing four…

VALVERT:

Enough waffle, sir.

CYRANO:
I'll create it as we duel and when the last
Line comes around — thrust home.

VALVERT: *(narky)*

Will you?

CYRANO:

I will.

(declaiming)
"Ballade of the Duel at the Hotel Bourgogne
Between de Bergerac and a Boetian."

VALVERT:
What's that supposed to mean?

CYRANO: *(with withering scorn)*

The title, m'sieur.

*(Tableau: A huddle of people forms in the center of the floor with the
MARQUIS and OFFICERS mingling with the citizens and others in the
inn. Some of the PAGES mount the shoulders of onlookers to get a better
view; in the boxes, the ladies raise their lorgnettes and lean over expectantly. DE GUICHE and his entourage are on the right LE BRET, CUIGY,
RAGUENEAU and others of CYRANO's persuasion, to the left.)*

A moment while I choose my rhymes.
*(CYRANO places two fingers to his brow and, with poetic concentration,
slowly shuts his eyes. Having consulted his Muse, he then opens them
wide.)*
Allons!
(Throughout, he suits the action to the word.)
First I doff my old chapeau,
My ancient cape (that's slightly frayed),
And as I measure up my foe,
I send my voice into my blade.

A Lancelot reborn am I,
Hear my saber swish and whoosh!
Like Spartacus, I twirl and fly
More agile I, than Scaramouche.
(They cross swords; the duel starts in earnest.)
Where shall I skewer this popinjay
(This poor misguided upstart crow)
In his bosom, shall we say;
In his belly or below?
Can you hear my saber's call
As I intone this jolly poem.
Now you're backed against the wall,
And soon enough, I will thrust home.
Your complexion's getting very pale
Your breathing's short, and it's my hunch
It's something indigestible
You may perchance have had for lunch.
(Beats down VALVERT's *sword with a two-handed blow.)*
Sorry for that sudden crunch
I didn't mean to hit your dome
We poets're such a rowdy bunch,
But soon enough, I will thrust home.
*(*CYRANO *throws some fast passes at his adversary which he parries with some difficulty, then stops abruptly and says with great solemnity:)*
O God, I fear the time has come
To end this fateful little poem.
The end is sad and rather glum.
With one last flourish…
(He lunges; VALVERT *staggers back and falls into the arms of his friends.* CYRANO *recovers, salutes.)*
                    I thrust home!

(Genial acclaim, cheers and stamping. Applause from the boxes; CYRANO *is pelted with flowers and handkerchiefs; the* OFFICERS *offer their congratulations.* RAGUENEAU, *unable to control his enthusiasm, dances with joy.* VALVERT's *friends help him stagger away.)*

A GUARDSMAN:
    Superb.

A WOMAN:
> Bravo!

RAGUENEAU:
>> You were magnificent.

1ST MARQUIS:
> Quite novel.

ANOTHER WOMAN:
>> Quite beautiful.

PAGE:
>>> Quite jolly.

LE BRET:
>>>> Quite mad!

A MUSKETEER: *(advancing with hand outstretched)*
> Allow me sir, to add my compliments.
> I know a little of the art myself
> And yet could not refrain from calling out
> My passionate approval!
> *(Bows and exits quickly.)*

CYRANO: (to CUIGY:)
>> Who was that?

CUIGY:
> A musketeer. His name is d'Artagnan.

LE BRET: *(taking CYRANO by the arm)*
> We must talk.

CYRANO:
>> First let the crowd disperse.
> *(to BELLEROSE)*
> May we stay?

BELLEROSE:
>> As long as you wish, M'sieur.

(Boos and catcalls are heard offstage.)

JODELET: *(coming from the door)*
> It's Montfleury. They're pelting him with garbage.

BELLEROSE: *(solemnly)*
> *Sic transit gloria.*
> *(shouting to the stage workers)*
>> Sweep the floors!

Shut the doors. But leave the lights alone.
After supper we begin rehearsals
For tonight's play.
(pointedly to CYRANO*)*
> It's a farce!

*(*JODELET *and* BELLEROSE *bow to* CYRANO *and Exeunt.)*

DOORKEEPER: *(to* CYRANO*)*
Do you not dine, Cyrano?
CYRANO:
> I? — No.

(The DOORKEEPER *moves out.)*

LE BRET:
Because?
CYRANO: *(haughty)*
> Because…
(seeing the DOORKEEPER *has gone, he drops his hauteur)*
> Because I have no money.
LE BRET:
No money?
(miming the throwing of the purse)
> You threw that purse to Jodelet?
CYRANO:
My pension. — Whoosh! — Gone with a twist of the wrist.
LE BRET:
So you're left with…
CYRANO:
> Nothing.
LE BRET:
> What a folly!
CYRANO:
But a great *coup-de-theatre,* you must admit.
ORANGE GIRL: *(coughs to attract attention;* CYRANO *and* LE BRET *turn to her.)*
Pardon M'sieur, but everyone should have
Enough to eat. *(indicating sideboard)*

I have plenty. *(offering)* Please.

CYRANO: *(doffing his hat)*

My gracious child, my Gascon pride recoils
From acts of charity — yet to avoid
Offense, I'll venture to take
(examines the sideboard)

          a little grape.

(She offers him a bunch; he pulls off one.)
Just one. And this glass of water.
(She is about to pour in wine; he stops her.)

          Straight!

And… half a macaroon.
(He breaks one in two and returns the other half.)

LE BRET:

          You are a fool.

ORANGE GIRL:

But M'sieur — nothing more?

CYRANO:

          Why yes —

Your hand to kiss.
(He gently plants a kiss on the vendor's hand as if it were the hand of a princess.)

ORANGE GIRL:

          Thank you, sir. — Good night.

(She exits.)

CYRANO:

Now begin; I'm listening as I dine.
(Places himself before the sideboard and arranges the morsels before him.)
Dinner. — *(the macaroon)* Drink. — *(the water)*

          Dessert. *(the grape)*. You've no idea
How ravenous I am. *(eating)*

          — And so?

LE BRET:

These fat, belligerent fools with pompous airs
Will be the death of you — if you heed them.
You should consort with wiser folk and better
Your behavior.

CYRANO: *(polishing off the macaroon)*

          Really quite filling, you know.

LE BRET:
    Like the Cardinal, for instance.

CYRANO: *(beaming)*
                    Was he here?

LE BRET:
    He must have thought you quite…

CYRANO:
                          — original!
    He's a playwright himself, I understand,
    And being one is probably delighted
    To find that I've shut down the competition.

LE BRET:
    All you seem to do is make new enemies.

CYRANO: *(starting on the grape)*
    How many d'you think I've made today?

LE BRET:
    Excluding all the women. I would say:
    Forty-eight.

CYRANO:
            That many? Count them out.

LE BRET:
    Montfleury. Baro. De Guiche. Valvert,
    The Marquis and the whole of the Academy.

CYRANO:
    Enough! — You give me too much joy.

LE BRET:
                    But where
    Will all this lead? — What purpose does it serve?

CYRANO:
    I've wandered all my life on many roads,
    Wasting energy on countless plans.
    Now I've only one.

LE BRET:
            And that one is?

CYRANO:
    The simplest of the lot: that is: to be
    In all things and in every way, admirable.

LE BRET:
    Well then, let's begin with Montfleury.
    Tell me why you hate him. Truthfully.

CYRANO: *(rising)*
>This pig who cannot see beyond his paunch
>Still thinks himself a dashing ladies-man.
>And as he plays his part upon the stage,
>Throws amorous glances with his piggy eyes
>Upon the women in the gallery.
>I have loathed him ever since the day
>He dared to smile upon — O 'twas like
>A slimy little slug that slithered through
>The petals of a fragile rose.
>*(pause)*

LE BRET: *(quietly astonished)*
>   What?
>Is it possible that —

CYRANO: *(bitterly)*
>   I can love?
>*(becoming grimly serious)*
>Yes, I can love.

LE BRET:
>   And yet you've never breathed
>A word of it to me. — May I know —

CYRANO:
>Whom I love? — Consider for a moment;
>Consider carefully who and what I am.
>It is unthinkable that anyone,
>The plainest wretch, the lowest, meanest maid
>Would not despise this monstrous countenance;
>This nose which fiendishly precedes me by
>A quarter of an hour. — Now, I ask you
>Whom should such a monster love? — Of course,
>The fairest woman in the world.

LE BRET:
>   The fairest?

CYRANO:
>The fairest, gentlest, woman in the land.
>The loveliest hair, the keenest mind —

LE BRET:
>   But who,
>Who is she?

CYRANO:
>   And most dangerous
> Without meaning to be; exquisite, without
> Knowing she is. A decoy set by Nature
> To snare mankind. An innocent white rose
> In which love lies in ambush waiting for
> Its prey. And he who knows her smile has known
> Perfection. — She is holy like a seraph,
> But of her grace, she's wholly unaware.
> All of heaven seems contained within
> Her slightest little movement. Neither Venus
> Nestling in her shell nor Diana
> In her forest-glades are half-as-fair
> As when she lounges in a chair or treads
> The cobbled streets of Paris.

LE BRET:
>   I think I know
> Of whom you speak.

CYRANO:
>   — Is it that transparent?

LE BRET:
> Your cousin, Madeleine Robin.

CYRANO: *(softly)*
>   Roxane.

LE BRET: *(after a beat)*
> If you love her, tell her so. Today
> You steeped yourself in glory and within
> Her very presence.

CYRANO:
>   O look me in the face
> Dear friend. What kind of chance have I
> With this protuberance between my eyes?
> I have no illusions. — Even though
> I must admit I sometimes fantasize,
> Walking in the evening through the bower
> With the raindrops drying on the leaves,
> Inhaling April's fragrance through these nostrils;
> Watching lovers strolling arm in arm
> And yearning for a woman of my own
> To fondle gently underneath the moon,

Bantering and trading tender phrases.
I lose myself within this reverie
Until I glimpse the shadow of my profile
Mocking me upon the garden-wall.
LE BRET: *(feelingly)*
My friend…
CYRANO: *(drooping)*
       I have my hours of desolation
Knowing myself so ugly and alone,
And sometimes… *(pause)*
LE BRET:
      You weep.
CYRANO: *(rallying)*
        No, never that!
That would be more monstrous still. To think
That tears would trickle down the winding alleys
Of this nose! — So long as I'm its master
I'll not permit my pity to profane
The dignity of sorrow. Never tears!
There is nothing more sublime than tears.
I will not demean them with my pathos.
LE BRET:
Love is only chance, my friend.
CYRANO:
      I dote
On Cleopatra, but I am not Caesar;
Love Eloise, but am not Abelard.
LE BRET:
But you have wit and courage, style and flair.
This little girl just now who offered food:
She too had eyes and didn't turn away.
CYRANO:
That is true.
LE BRET:
    And Roxane herself
Watching as you dueled grew pale.
CYRANO:
      Grew pale?
LE BRET:
Her heart and spirit are already touched.

Take your courage in both hands and speak;
Speak to her.
CYRANO:

        And hear her laugh at me?
Of all the things on earth, that do I fear
The most.
DOORKEEPER: *(ushering in the DUENNA)*

        A lady M'sieur who asks for you.
CYRANO: *(startled)*

It is her Duenna —
DUENNA: *(reverently)*

Our good cousin would be pleased to know
Someplace where we might have a private word.
CYRANO:

With me?
DUENNA:

        With you indeed, good sir. There are
Certain things my lady would impart.
CYRANO:

Certain…
DUENNA:

        … things I say, the lady would impart.
CYRANO: *(trembling)*

Heavens!
DUENNA:

        She will tomorrow, at first flush
Of dawn, be in St. Roch for morning mass.
CYRANO: *(supporting himself on LE BRET)*

At morning mass?
DUENNA:

        And after that, is there
Some place perhaps, where you can meet and talk?
CYRANO: *(befuddled)*

And talk — can meet and talk?
DUENNA:

        Well answer, sir!
CYRANO: *(gruff)*

I'm thinking.
DUENNA: *(sarcastic)*

        That's a start.

CYRANO:

Ragueneau's!
The pastry cook. — The shop of Ragueneau.

DUENNA:

Which is?

CYRANO:

The pastry shop of Ragueneau!

DUENNA: *(impatiently)*

Which *is?*

CYRANO: *(finally twigging)*
On the Rue
(trying to remember)
— Oh God
— St. Honorè.

DUENNA: *(mechanically repeating)*
'The Rue — O God — St. Honorè.' She will
Be there at seven.

CYRANO:

At seven!?

DUENNA: *(vexed by his repetitions)*

Good afternoon.

(Exits.)

CYRANO: *(collapsing into LE BRET's arms)*
To see me!

LE BRET:

Well, your spirits are improved.

CYRANO:

That means at least, she knows that I'm alive.

LE BRET:

And now you will be calm.

CYRANO:

I will be — will *be* —
Full of fire and frenzy, a raging storm.
I need to fight a regiment! I've spawned
A dozen hearts — a hundred arms. No mortal
Foes for me, O let me battle giants!

(During the last speeches, the shadows of actors preparing to rehearse have been visible at the back of the stage. Now the musicians enter, take their places and the rehearsal proper begins.)

A VOICE FROM THE STAGE:
Quiet down there. — This is a rehearsal.

CYRANO:

We're off.

(As he turns upstage, CUIGY, BRISSAILLE and others enter carrying LIGNIERE who is totally inebriated.)

CUIGY:
Cyrano!

CYRANO:
What's this.

CUIGY:
The prodigal's returned.

CYRANO:
Ligniere, what's happened?

BRISSAILLE: *(explaining to CYRANO)*
He's afraid to go home.

CYRANO:
But why?

LIGNIERE: *(with a thick voice, unfolding a crumpled note)*
You see, a hundred to one, and *I'm* the one!
And all because of a song. — A hundred men —
Waiting to get me — at the Porte de Nesle.
On my way home. — Let me stay the night
With you.

CYRANO: *(after a beat)*
Only a hundred. Is that all? —
You *shall* go home, Ligniere.

LIGNIERE: *(like a baby)*
But I don't *want* to!

CYRANO: *(with grim determination, he points to the lantern being held by the DOORKEEPER.)*
The lantern! Take it!

(LIGNIERE involuntarily reacting to CYRANO's command, briskly snatches it from the DOORKEEPER)

Now, forward! March, I say.
I shall be your guardian tonight

And you've my word, no harm will come to you.
(to the officers)
And all you others, follow hard upon.
This spectacle must have an audience.
CUIGY:
    But a hundred to one!
CYRANO:
                I'll take no lesser odds.

(The performers, in various stages of undress, hearing the commotion approach the stage.)

LE BRET:
    Why risk your life…
CYRANO:
              There's that noise again:
    Le Bret lecturing!
LE BRET:
             …for this drunkard!
CYRANO:
    Because this drunkard, this cask of muscatel,
    This barrel of brandy, once committed an act
    Of peerless beauty. For one day, after Mass,
    Seeing his beloved being blessed
    With holy water, scampered to the font,
    And, though he cannot bear the taste of water,
    Scooped it up and straight 'way drank it down.
A SOUBRETTE:
    Now that I think is truly an act of love.
CYRANO:
    Indeed it is: a sacred act of love.
A SOUBRETTE: *(to the others)*
    But why should five score men so set upon
    One single harmless poet?
CYRANO: *(to the officers)*
                I say, march!
    And heed me well, whatever threat there be,
    Let no man come to my aid.
ANOTHER ACTRESS: *(leaping off the stage)*
              I'm going as well!

CYRANO:
Welcome. — It's free of charge.
YET ANOTHER ACTRESS: *(to an old character actress)*
And you, Cassandra?
CYRANO:
Come one, come all! Dottore, Isabel,
Leander — the full company! We'll transform
Commedia d'el Arte into Spanish tragedy.
With ribbons, banners, masks and mandolins
We'll jangle like a frantic tambourine.
THE ACTRESSES:
Bravo! — My cloak! — My gown! — My shawl!
JODELET:
Allons!
CYRANO: *(to the violinists)*
And you shall play the grand accompaniment.

(The violinists join the spontaneous procession. Lit candles are taken from the footlights and passed out among the revelers, turning them into a torchlight procession.)

(like a drill sergeant)
Fall in! Cadets to the front. Actors behind!
And at the head of the column, — myself!
Alone, and wreathed in glory like Ulysses
Ready to storm the ancient walls of Troy.
Remember — no one's to lift a hand to help me!
Are we ready? —

(The troops shout their assent.)

One…two…three:
Throw open the door!

(The DOORKEEPER, very much in the spirit of the occasion, dramatically swings open the great doors of the Hall. In the moonlight, we can just barely glimpse a segment of Paris glowing in the distance.)

Paris lies before us
Wearing its evening haze like a negligee.

The moonlight bounces off the slanting roofs.
Nature's elegantly set the scene.
And there beneath the hanging mist, the Seine,
Sparkling like a shard of polished glass.
And what shall be, shall be.

ALL:

                        Onward, onward!

To the Porte de Nesle!

CYRANO: *(turning to the SOUBRETTE)*
You asked before why a hundred swords
Are drawn against one measly little poet.
(drawing his own sword)
Because they know this man's a friend of *mine!*

(CYRANO exits, the procession following close behind. LIGNIERE, in his stupor is staggering at its head, then the OFFICERS, the ACTRESSES and other members of the Company, some of whom leap and dance to the sound of the violins which have struck up a martial air — all illuminated by the flickering candles held high in the marchers' hands.)

CURTAIN

Act II

A grand emporium of bread and cakes belonging to RAGUENEAU. Situated on the corner of Rue St. Honorè and the Rue de l' Arbre Sec which, through the first light of dawn, are just barely visible through the glass panels on the door at the back.

Downstage and to the Left is a long counter above which looms a wrought-iron canopy. Ducks, geese and white peacocks hang from it. Bouquets of flowers, particularly large sunflowers, fan out of great Oriental vases. On the same side, there is a second entrance, a great fireplace and, on the andirons in between, saucepans into which the roasts are dripping. There is a door Stage Right; at the second entrance, a staircase leading to a small loft, the interior of the room just visible through open blinds. There we can discern a small private diningroom with table and a Flemish candlestick already lit. From the head of the stairway, a wooden gallery seems to lead off to similar small rooms.

In the center of the shop hangs an iron ring which can be raised or lowered by a rope. It is decorated with the heads of large game and somewhat resembles a kind of culinary chandelier.

Beneath the staircase, we can see the glow of the ovens. The copper pots and pans glisten. The spits revolve. Hams hang from the rafters. There are great piles of fancy pastry on every side. The morning baking ritual is in full swing. Tall cooks, busy scullions and scurrying apprentices, their white caps peaked with chicken feathers, move in a kind of mechanistic pantomime throughout the shop. A variety of sumptuous pastries and cakes are carried to and fro on wicker trays and metal foils. Some tables already contain assortments of pastry; others await their customers. In one corner there is a small table barely visible under an avalanche of paper; there RAGUENEAU sits pen in hand, composing poetry.

1ST PASTRY COOK: *(carrying in a dish)*
    Fruit-flan.
2ND PASTRY COOK: *(with dish)*
    Candied fruits.

3RD PASTRY COOK: *(carrying roast decorated with feathers)*
 Peacock surprise!
4TH PASTRY COOK: *(with tray)*
 Sweetmeats Ragueneau!
5TH PASTRY COOK: *(carrying it in a pan)*
 Beef en casserole.
RAGUENEAU: *(stops writing and raises his head)*
 The silver light of dawn begins to glisten
 On my copper pots, so silence Muse,
 Come back another time. Homer departs
 When the ovens beckon.
 (dips his finger into a sauce)
        Too much cream.
THE COOK:
 How much too much?
RAGUENEAU: *(demonstrating on a digit of his finger)*
       This much, too much.
1ST PASTRY COOK:
          The rolls?
RAGUENEAU: *(taking one and sitting before the fireplace)*
 Avert thine eyes O gentle Muse, or else
 My wafting kitchen fumes will clog thy sight.
 (tossing the roll back to the PASTRY COOK)
 You've cut these bloody rolls all wrong. Perpend!
 An equal hemstitch on each side and a
 Caesura in the middle.
 (snatching an unfinished piece of pastry from another)
        This house of crust
 Needs a sugared roof to make it firm!
 (to another, placing fowls upon a spit)
 And you, my boy, upon the circling spit
 Should place the pullet and the browning turkey
 Alternately, as the old Malherbe
 Juxtaposes lengthy lines of verse
 With shorter ones containing female rhymes.
 A tasty roast, should be as well turned as
 A couplet.
APPRENTICE: *(coming forward with a covered platter)*
      Master, I've prepared this dish
 Expressly with the thought of you in mind.

I hope it pleases.
(removes the napkin revealing a lyre made entirely out of pastry)
RAGUENEAU: *(dazzled)*

Ah, an ancient lyre.

APPRENTICE:

In pastry…
RAGUENEAU:

And trellised round with candied fruit.

APPRENTICE:

And see, the strings are all spun sugar.
RAGUENEAU:

Mon dieu,

A little masterpiece. *(touched, gives him money)*
Go drink my health!

(LISE enters.)

Shh — my wife — just go about your work
And hide that money. —
(shows the lyre to LISE, underplaying his enthusiasm)
Quite charming, no?

LISE: *(grouchily)*

No!

(Placing a pile of paper bags on the counter.)
RAGUENEAU:

Bags? I thank you —
(looks at them more closely)
What's this? My manuscripts!

The verses of my friends, all cut to pieces!
Turned into a pile of bags for pastry!
(turning his wrath on her)
You are no better than the wild Bacchantes
Who tormented Orpheus.
LISE:

Why not?

Why shouldn't I employ those useless scraps
For something practical? They've eaten us out
Of house and home and never paid a sou!
RAGUENEAU:

Gad! would you admonish owls for hooting?

50

LISE:

> *I* don't give a hoot! — Before these moles
> Came digging in our kitchens, nor did you!
> You didn't talk of 'Bacchantes' then and spend
> Your time composing drivel.

RAGUENEAU:

> What, my verses
>
> Drivel?

LISE:

> Useless, pointless doggerel!

(Two children enter the shop. RAGUENEAU takes the opportunity to divert his anger.)

RAGUENEAU:

> What will it be, my dears?

1ST CHILD:

> Three patties, please.

RAGUENEAU:

> There you are — all hot and brown.

2ND CHILD:

> But could you
>
> Put them in a bag for us?

RAGUENEAU: *(painfully)*

> A bag.
> *(As he is about to place them into one of his 'literary' bags, he reads the wrapper.)*
> "Ulysses when he left Penelope…"
> No, not that one.
> *(goes for another)*
> "Phoebus with his crown of gold…"
> Oh no, I couldn't.
> *(puts it aside)*

LISE:

> Well, get on with it!

RAGUENEAU: *(takes a third then, with resignation)*

> The sonnet to Phyllis. — Well, if I must, I must!

LISE:

> What a performance — over a little bag!

RAGUENEAU: *(As LISE's back is turned, he secretively beckons the children back.)*

Give me back that sonnet, give it here!
— I'll give you six patties for your three.

(The children return the bag, snatch the extra cakes and run off.
RAGUENEAU *smooths out the paper bag and begins to recite the sonnet*
printed thereon.)

'O sweet Phyllis…!" Damn! A splodge of butter
On her name!
CYRANO: *(entering hurriedly)*
           Tell me, what's the time?
RAGUENEAU:
    Just six.
CYRANO:
        An hour more.
RAGUENEAU:
                   Congratulations!
CYRANO:
    For what?
RAGUENEAU:
         Your duel?
CYRANO:
              Which one?
RAGUENEAU:
                   Hotel de Bourgogne.
The one you fought in rhyme.
CYRANO:
                  Ancient history.
LISE:
    He's talked of nothing else.
CYRANO:
              Alot of nonsense.
RAGUENEAU: *(taking up a serving spoon as a foil)*
    'With one last flourish, I thrust home!' — Superb!
A short suspenseful phrase: — 'with one last flourish'
Then the little button: — 'I thrust home!'
CYRANO:
    What's the time now?

RAGUENEAU:

Six past one.

(thrusting home)

Whoosh!

And in perfect ballade form.

LISE: *(having mechanically shaken his hand, suddenly examines it)*

What's happened?

CYRANO:

My hand? — Oh nothing, a trifle.

RAGUENEAU:

You've been hurt.

CYRANO:

A little scratch.

LISE:

If you ask me he's lying.

CYRANO: *(confiding in RAGUENEAU)*

I'm expecting someone. — Leave us alone
When they arrive.

RAGUENEAU:

But any moment now

My poets will be here.

LISE: *(grumpily)*

To feed their faces!

CYRANO:

Take them out — when I give you the sign.—
What's the time?

RAGUENEAU:

Ten minutes after.

CYRANO:

A pen!

(RAGUENEAU hands him the one stuck behind his ear as a MUSKETEER with an oversize moustache and a stentorian manner enters and addresses LISE.)

MUSKETEER:

Bonjour Lise.

CYRANO:

Who's that?

RAGUENEAU:

> A friend of my wife's,
> A very gallant swordsman — so they say.

CYRANO: *(clutching the pen and waving RAGUENEAU away)*

> Write it — fold it — hand it to her and flee.
> *(tosses down the pen.)*
> What craven cowardice! — But I'll be damned
> If I can speak a single word to her —
> What's the time? —

RAGUENEAU:

> A quarter past.

CYRANO:

> — of all
> The words I've locked in here. *(strikes his chest)*
> But if I write —
> *(takes up the pen again)*
> I'll write it out. The letter I've composed
> A thousand times before and never sent,
> Never even penned, and yet I know
> Each and every word of it by heart.

(As he writes, we see, through the glass doors behind, a bevy of shadowy figures. A motley collection of poets, dressed in black, their clothes splattered with mud, enter.)

LISE:

> Your scarecrows have arrived.

1ST POET:

> Comrade!

2ND POET: *(Taking RAGUENEAU's hands)*

> Brother.

3RD POET:

> Peerless pastry cook, *(sniffs)* — divine aroma!

4TH POET:

> Great Phoebus of the apple tarts, Salut!

5TH POET:

> Hail, Apollo of the Grand Eclair! —

(RAGUENEAU is surrounded, embraced and jovially thumped upon the back.)

RAGUENEAU:
>How one quickly feels at ease among
>One's own.

1ST POET:
>   The debris at the Porte de Nesle
>Have made us late.

2ND POET:
>   A heap of wounded men
>All bruised and bleeding, strewn upon the street:
>Eight of the meanest pigs you've ever seen.

CYRANO: *(suddenly distracted)*
>Eight? — I'd have sworn there were only seven.
>*(returns to his letter)*

RAGUENEAU:
>D' you know the man responsible for this mayhem?

CYRANO:
>I? No.

LISE: *(to the haughty Musketeer)*
>   Do you?

MUSKETEER: *(sly, twisting his moustachioes)*
>   Perhaps I do.

1ST POET:
>One man alone, they say, put them all
>To rout.

2ND POET:
>   And what a bloody sight it was!
>Swords, pikes, daggers, bludgeons…

CYRANO: *(immersed in his letter)*
>   "Your eyes…"

3RD POET:
>Hats, scarves, belts, buckles…

CYRANO:
>   "Your lips…"

3RD POET:
>— scattered everywhere. A man like that…

1ST POET:
>Must be a holy terror…

CYRANO:
>   "…your fair tresses"

3RD POET:
> Only a heartless savage could have done it.

CYRANO:
> "And I grow faint when I confront your beauty…"

2ND POET:
> What are you writing now, Ragueneau?

CYRANO:
> "Your friend, who loves you" — No, no signature.
> I'll deliver it in person.

RAGUENEAU: *(to the 2ND POET)*
> A recipe in rhyming couplets.

3RD POET:
>   Show!
> Let's have a look. Don't keep it to yourself.

4TH POET: *(munching as he speaks)*
> This brioche is cocking its cap at me.

1ST POET: This naughty little cake is making eyes
> At me, I do believe. *(biting into it)* Ma cherie!

2ND POET:
> Well Ragueneau, we all attend.

3RD POET: *(licking cream out of a muffin)*
>   Shameless,
> The way these brazen eclairs dribble cream!

1ST POET: *(taking a great bite out of the lyre of pastry)*
> The first time that a lyre's actually fed me.

RAGUENEAU: *(coughing as into his formal recitation)*
> A recipe in rhyme.

2ND POET: *(nudging 1ST POET)*
>   Breakfeast?

1ST POET:
>   No, dinner.

RAGUENEAU:
> "The Mystery of Almond Cream Tarts."
> Take your eggs and beat them lightly
> Add a pinch of salt but slightly.
> When it's mixed and really fluffy
> Squeeze in a bit of lemon juice and almond cream,
>   mix briskly with a wooden ladle
>   for three full minutes in a counter-
>   clockwise direction until the whole

is pure and puffy.
Then add the pastry merrily
With nuts (not necessarily)
Then pour the fluffy cream quite thickly,
Adding sugar, spice, lard, poppy seeds, vanilla
        beans, custard, honey, arrowroot,
        cornstarch and cinnamon until the
        mix is fairly thick and sickly.
Once you've got it nice and frothy
Then let it heat within its potty,
Until it's baked and simmering
And voila, — almond tarts fit for a king!

THE POETS:
Charming! Scrumptious! Delicious! Delectable!

(In a frenzy of appreciation, the POETS scoop buns, tarts, eclairs and other assorted pastry into their mouths, incomprehensibly spouting superlatives for RAGUENEAU's verse.)

CYRANO: *(who has watched the whole spectacle)*
Do you not see these vultures feeding on
Your good nature?

RAGUENEAU:
            I see, but turn aside
My glance, lest it should irritate my friends.
My little verses give me, as it were,
A double pleasure: allow me to indulge
My weakness for the art, while feeding those
Who without my aid, might hungry go.

CYRANO: *(slaps him on the back)*
You're a silly ass...
(aside, as he turns away)
           — but a good soul.
(calling to LISE)
Madame, this haughty musketeer lays siege
Upon your heart, n'est ce pas?

LISE:
              I can with one
Sharp and withering look protect my virtue
From all who would assail it.

CYRANO: *(looking at her sternly)*

> P'raps, and yet
It seems to me quite vulnerable to attack.

(LISE looks guilty at CYRANO.)

(now raising his voice so the MUSKETEER can hear)
Ragueneau's a friend of mine and so
I shall not suffer anyone who makes
Him out to be a fool.
LISE: *(offended)*

> You think that I —
CYRANO:

A word to the wise is sufficient, so they say.
(turning to the MUSKETEER who quakes at his glance)
Let's hope the maxim's true.

(He salutes the MUSKETEER abruptly, almost as if he were going for his sword. The MUSKETEER involuntarily recoils, then lamely returns CYRANO's salute.)

LISE: *(to the MUSKETEER)*

> You take all that!?
You should've tweaked him by the nose.
MUSKETEER:

> His nose?

Have you *seen* it?

(The MUSKETEER, trembling visibly, exits hurriedly, LISE in tow.)

(ROXANE and the DUENNA appear outside the door. CYRANO immediately signals to RAGUENEAU who proceeds to lure away the Poets.)

RAGUENEAU:
We shall find it much more comfortable
In here good friends, for reading poetry.
1ST POET:
But the cakes?
RAGUENEAU:

> We'll take them all along.

(Sweeping up as much as of them as they can carry, they and the pastry follow RAGUENEAU into the other room.)

CYRANO: *(clutching his letter)*
If there's the faintest chance then I'll…
(Throws open the doors, bows.)
                Welcome!

(As ROXANE enters, CYRANO takes the DUENNA to one side.)

May I have one word.
DUENNA:
             Take two, m'sieur.
CYRANO:
How is your appetite, in general?
DUENNA:
                  Quite good.
CYRANO:
Here 're two sonnets by a local poet.
DUENNA:
                  Sonnets?
CYRANO:
Filled up to the brim with these eclairs.
(fills up bag)
DUENNA: *(salivating)*
Eclairs!?
CYRANO:
      D'you like cream puffs?
DUENNA:
              I'm rather partial.
CYRANO:
I'll empty six within the bosom of
This triolet by Saint-Amant. And in
This ode by Chapelian, a scrumptious piece
Of sponge cake dipped in Elderberry wine!
DUENNA: *(secretively)*
I must confess to some small passion for
Patisserie.
CYRANO: *(piling the cakes into her arms)*
      Indulge it, sweet-toothed madam.

But prefer'bly outside.

DUENNA:

Outside? But I —

CYRANO: *(gently coaxing her out)*

Make sure you swallow every single mouthful.

(Closes the door behind her, returns to ROXANE *and respectfully doffs his hat.)*

Now blessed be this blessed hour at which

You've come to tell me...tell me... tell me what?

ROXANE: *(removing her mask)*

First to render thanks — for that dolt

Whom you routed with your sword. His patron,

Who thinks himself in love with me, would press

That foolish knave upon me for a husband.

CYRANO:

I fought then not for the honour of my nose

But your bright eyes: a far more noble aim.

ROXANE: And then to also tell you — though I wonder —

Do you still recall how like a brother

You were to me in those far distant days

When we played together in the park

Beside the lake.

CYRANO:

You used to come each year

To Bergerac.

ROXANE:

You fashioned swords then out

Of whittled wood.

CYRANO:

And you put dandelions

Upon your dolls to make their tresses blonde.

ROXANE:

Our days of childish play. Of picking plums...

CYRANO:

And gathering the mulberries from the bush.

ROXANE:

In those days, you did whate'er I asked.

CYRANO:

Roxane, in braids; we called you Madeleine,

ROXANE:
>   Was I pretty then?

CYRANO:
>   — Not unsightly.

ROXANE:
>   Do you remember when you'd cut your hand,
>   You came to me and I'd pretend to be
>   Mama — and speak in stern, maternal tones:
>   *(she takes his hand.)*
>   "What mischief are you up to now, dear boy?
>   What have you done to make your hand so —"
>   *(notices his cut, starts)*
>   What *have* you done to yourself? — At your age!

CYRANO: *(reverting to childishness)*
>   I was playing. — By the Porte de Nesle.
>   With quite few big boys.

ROXANE: *(wetting her handkerchief in water and applying it to his hand)*
>   Now just hold still.

CYRANO:
>   Such a doting mother. And so kind.

ROXANE:
>   Now tell me honestly and do not fib.
>   Just how many of those 'big boys' were there?

CYRANO:
>   About a hundred.

ROXANE:
>   A hundred men, good heavens!

CYRANO:
>   That doesn't matter now. But what were you
>   About to say. — Tell me, if you dare.

ROXANE: *(his hand still in hers)*
>   I think I do dare now. — Once I could
>   Tell you anything and now I think
>   I can again. — The thing is: I'm in love.

CYRANO: *(beat)*
>   In love.

ROXANE:
>   With one who doesn't know.

CYRANO:
>   Who doesn't —

ROXANE:

Not yet. But one who shortly will.

CYRANO: *(breathless)*

Shortly…

ROXANE:

A man who loves me too, but from afar;
Too shy to ever dare to speak his love.
Your hand is fev'rish.
(she continues to bind it.)

And yet I know he wants to.

I've sensed it in his eyes.
(finishes the bandaging)

There, that's better.

And he's a soldier too. In fact, in your
Own regiment. — In your own company.
And heaven, what a man he is! Strong,
Proud, noble, young, beautiful.

CYRANO: *(involuntarily withdrawing his hand)*

Beautiful?

ROXANE:

What's wrong?

CYRANO:

Nothing. My hand. A little twinge.

ROXANE:

Well, I love him madly, and I've never
Seen him anywhere except the playhouse.

CYRANO:

You haven't spoken?

ROXANE:

Only with our eyes.

CYRANO:

How can you know —?

ROXANE:

I've heard the others talking —
The gossip — and I know — I simply know.

CYRANO:

You say he's in my regiment.

ROXANE:

He is.

CYRANO:

 His name?

ROXANE:

    Baron Christian de Neuvillette.

CYRANO:

 There's no one by that name.

ROXANE:

        Since this morning!

 Under the command of Captain Carbon

 De Castel-Jaloux.

CYRANO: *(studying her)*

      How carelessly we fling

 Our hearts away. — Now listen, my dear child —

DUENNA: *(entering)*

 Monsieur de Bergerac, I've finished every

 One of your sweet cakes.

CYRANO:

      Now read the verses!

 (He briskly wheels the DUENNA out again.)

 My dear child, have you considered deeply?

 You, who dote on language, wit and poetry.

 Why for all you know, the man may be

 An unlettered savage.

ROXANE:

     It couldn't be.

 He's so handsome; he has curls like one

 Of d'Urfè's heroes.

CYRANO:

     Yet his speech may lag

 Behind his fine coiffure.

ROXANE:

       Oh no, I'm sure

 He's as brilliant as he's beautiful.

 His soul is in his eyes.

CYRANO:

      And yet his brains

 May be in his boots. — What if behind

 That fine facade, there lurks a simple dolt?

ROXANE:

 Then I shall die.

CYRANO: *(after a pause)*
      And this is what you had
 To tell me. — I don't understand, madame,
 Why I should be your special confidante.
ROXANE:
 Yesterday, I heard that all are Gascons
 In your company — every single one —
CYRANO:
 And that we pick a quarrel with any man
 Who gains entrance to our regiment
 And is not Gascon through-and-through. Is that
 What you've heard?
ROXANE:
         Imagine how I feared
 For him on hearing that.
CYRANO: *(with gritted teeth)*
           As well you should!
ROXANE:
 And then I thought… you who were so brave,
 And yesterday, so fearless in that duel,
 If you, that all men held in awe…
CYRANO:
          Might come
 To the aid of your defenseless baron?
ROXANE:
 You will protect him for me, will you not?
 I have always been your friend…
CYRANO:
        You have.
ROXANE:
 Will you be *his* for my sake?
CYRANO:
      Be his *friend*…?!
ROXANE:
 And never ever let him fight a duel.
CYRANO: *(incensed)*
 Never let him fight a duel!?
ROXANE:
        — For me.

CYRANO: *(mechanically agreeing)*
    'And never let him fight a duel.' — Agreed.
ROXANE:
    Oh you are dear — a true and faithful friend.
    Now I must go. — Oh you never finished
    About last night. How terrible it must
    Have been. — Do have him write and tell me all
    About it. *(throws him a kiss)*
            I 'm so very fond of you.
CYRANO:
    Yes…yes…
ROXANE:
          A hundred men against just one!
    Incredible. — We are good friends, aren't we?
CYRANO:
    Yes…yes.
ROXANE:
          Do plead with him to write a letter.
    A hundred? — you must tell me all about it
    One day when I have more time. — What courage! *(She exits.)*
CYRANO: *(saluting her as she leaves)*
    I have shown much greater courage since.

(CYRANO stands motionless after the door has closed, his eyes fixed on the ground. After a leaden, anguished silence, the door on the right opens and RAGUENEAU's head appears.)

RAGUENEAU:
    May we come in?

(CYRANO, still motionless, nods 'yes.' RAGUENEAU and his friends flood back into the shop. At the same time, CARBON DE CASTEL-JALOUX enters from the street door. He is strong and distinguished-looking, wears the uniform of the Captain of the Guards and acknowledges CYRANO with a long, sweeping bow.)

CARBON:
          Ah, the conquering hero.
CYRANO: *(raising his head and saluting)*
    Mon Capitain.

CARBON:

        — We've heard all about it.

The regiment is just outside.

CYRANO: *(recoiling)*

        But I ——

CARBON:

To offer their congratulations!

CYRANO:

        But I...

CARBON: *(trying to cajole him out)*

They're just across the street inside the tavern.

(CYRANO still does not budge. CARBON calls to the men outside.)

He will not come. — No way! — Don't ask me why.

It seems he's in some funny sort of humor.

(Outside there is a great tumult of clanging swords and trampling feet as the troops converge upon the pastry shop. In a moment, they have all burst in shouting assorted Gascon oaths and exclamations: "Mille dious!" — "Capedious!" — "Mordious" — "Pocapdedious!" etc.)

RAGUENEAU: *(frightened by the tumult)*

Gentlemen, are you all Gascons?

THE CADETS:

        We are.

1ST CADET: *(to CYRANO)*

Bravo!

CYRANO: *(acknowledging him)*

    Baron!

2ND CADET: *(shaking both hands)*

        Excellent!

CYRANO: *(acknowledging him)*

        Baron!

3RD CADET: *(embracing him)*

        Lovely man!

CYRANO: *(acknowledging him)*

    Baron!

RAGUENEAU:

    Gracious, are you all barons?

CADETS:
> We are!

1ST CADET:
>> If we all wore our coronets
>> Our glitter would outshine the heavens.

LE BRET: *(entering hurriedly, to CYRANO)*
>>> Cyrano!
> A giant crowd, the whole town practically,
> Is looking for you everywhere. They've heard
> About last night.

CYRANO: *(fearful)*
>> You haven't said —

LE BRET: *(rubbing his hands together gleefully)*
>>> I have!

TRADESMAN:
> Stand back. The whole of Paris is outside!

(Indeed a great horde of people immediately try to burst through the doors of the pastry shop. Carriages and sedan-chairs choke the entrance-way.)

LE BRET: *(aside to CYRANO)*
> And Roxane?

CYRANO:
>> Shhh!

CROWD:
>> Cyrano! Cyrano! Cyrano!

(The mob bursts into the shop, shouting, cheering, howling.)

RAGUENEAU: *(jumping onto a table)*
(hysterical)
> Look at them! — Shrieking, howling, stamping!
(suddenly appreciative)
>>> Gorgeous, isn't it?

SEVERAL MEN:
> My friend! Good friend! Comrade!

CYRANO:
>> Who'd've guessed
> Yesterday I had so many friends.

LE BRET:
    Today you are a hero.
1ST MARQUIS: *(rushing to him with outstretched hands)*
                        My dear fellow.
CYRANO: *(coldly)*
    Yesterday, you weren't quite so amorous.
2ND MARQUIS:
    I have two ladies in my coach outside
    Whom I would like to introduce.
CYRANO:
                                But who
    Will introduce you to *me*, m'sieur.
LE BRET: *(to Cyrano)*
    What's got into you?
CYRANO:
                    Be quiet, Le Bret.
JOURNALIST: *(with pen and paper)*
    May I have a quote?
CYRANO:
                    You certainly may not.
LE BRET:
    Theophraste Renaudot — of the Gazette.
    Why he can 'make' you?
CYRANO:
                    Make me yawn, perhaps.
A POET: *(pushing forward)*
    M'sieur…m'sieur…
CYRANO:
                    What now?
A POET:
                        A pentacrostic.
CYRANO:
    Pardon.
A POET:
            I'd like to make a pentacrostic
    Of your name, m'sieur.
CYRANO: *(turning away)*
                    Nincompoop!

(The crowd surges backward to allow DE GUICHE, accompanied by

*CUIGY and BRISSAILLE to appear. They are surrounded by the same offi-
cers who were with CYRANO at the end of Act I.)*

CUIGY: *(To CYRANO)*
Monsieur de Guiche.

(The crowd stirs expectantly.)

                        Who brings a message from
Marshal de Gassion.
DE GUICHE:
                        Who, hearing of your affair,
Bids me convey his warmest compliments.

(The crowd lets out a rousing cheer.)

CYRANO: *(doffing his hat)*
We must attend when the Marshall speaks.
DE GUICHE:
Though skeptical at first, he soon received
Firsthand reports from those who swore they'd seen
It all —
CUIGY:
                With our own eyes!
LE BRET: *(aside, to CYRANO)*
                        What's wrong?
CYRANO:
Shhh.
LE BRET:
        There's something wrong. Are you in pain?
CYRANO: *(recovering)*
In pain? At such a moment. Really, Le Bret.
(His moustache bristles; he throws out his chest.)
Among a crowd like this. *(aside)* I'll tell you later.
DE GUICHE:
Your reputation's gone before you, sir.
You're one of these Gascons, are you not?
A CADET: *(proudly)*
He is indeed!

2ND CADET:

> As all of us proudly are!

DE GUICHE: *(surveying all the Gascons grouped behind CYRANO)*

> I see, then all these haughty gentlemen
> Are the famous —

CARBON:

> Cyrano!

CYRANO:

> Captain!

CARBON:

> Since it seems that all our men are present
> And accounted for, I think it meet
> We present them to the Comte de Guiche.

CYRANO: *(On a command, the CADETS immediately form into ranks before their CAPTAIN. CYRANO formally takes two paces forward to DE GUICHE and begins.)*

> Behold the Sons of Gascony
> Of Carbon de Castel-Jaloux.
> Who march to meet their destiny.
> A hard-fighting, hard-drinking crew.
> The brawling brothers of Gascony.
> Upholding the values of chivalry.
> Defending the old and the new.
> Unstoppable soldiers of Gascony
> Of Carbon de Castel-Jaloux.
> With eye of hawk and beak of eagle
> And wolf's bloodcurdling howl
> They rout the nation's enemies,
> Wherever they may prowl.
> They march in ranks, their heads held high
> Their swords are at the ready.
> With eye of hawk and beak of eagle
> Their nerves alert and steady.
> Breakers of skulls, breakers of pates,
> Blood's their favorite brew.
> Strong their loves; strong their hates,
> Gascons through and through.
> When quarrels come they're ready
> To see the quarrel through.
> Breakers of skulls, breakers of pates,

Blood's their favorite brew.
Behold the sons of Gascony
Who, playing at amorous sport,
Subdue all firm resistance
And win every woman they court.
In France, in Spain, in Italy.
The stouthearted sons of the nation
Besiege the heart of women
And cuckold the male population.
Behold the Sons of Gascony
As free with their purse as their lives
And when you see them on the march,
Best lock up all your wives.

DE GUICHE: *(seated in an armchair RAGUENEAU has provided)*
Poets are very much in vogue today,
Would you like to belong to my regiment?

CYRANO:
I belong to no one but myself, m'sieur
Wherever I may serve.

DE GUICHE:
Your rhyming duel
Yesterday amused my uncle the Cardinal.
I might be useful there.

LE BRET: *(impressed)*
What, Richelieu?

DE GUICHE:
I assume you have a verse-play up your sleeve;
Almost everyone has.

LE BRET: *(delighted)*
Your 'Agrippine'!
At last you'll have it performed.

DE GUICHE:
I'll show it him.

CYRANO: *(visibly tempted)*
My play —

DE GUICHE:
He's a dramatist himself.
A few revisions here and there and, Voila!
He'll make it ready for the stage.

71

CYRANO:

> Impossible!
> My blood runs cold to contemplate the change
> Of even one scintilla.

DE GUICHE:

> The Cardinal, you know
> Pays handsomely, should he decide to buy.

CYRANO:

> Not half so dear as I reward myself
> For the joy of writing what I please.

DE GUICHE:

> You are proud, m'sieur.

CYRANO:

> How observant
> Of you to notice.

(A CADET storms in holding a drawn sword upon which are impaled an assortment of bedraggled hats, tattered brims and wilted plumes.)

CADET:

> Cyrano, look at this!
> We found these all along the street this morning.
> The remnants of the fleeing popinjays
> You routed there last night.

CARBON:

> The spoils of war.

(the soldiers laugh)

CUIGY:

> Whoever put together such a band
> Of cutthroats must be furious today.

BRISSAILLE:

> I wonder who though it can be...

DE GUICHE:

> Myself!

(The laugher suddenly subsides. All turn to DE GUICHE.)

> Engaged to do the kind of work that one
> Doesn't stoop to do oneself: To take
> A cocky rhymester and bring him down a peg.

CADET: *(to CYRANO, of the remnants)*
> What'll we do with them? Put 'em in a stew?
> They're greasy enough.

CYRANO: *(Taking the sword, he makes a salute causing the remnants to slide down the blade and fall in a heap at the feet of DE GUICHE.)*
> Pray, return these to their rightful owners?
> I assume you do not want them for yourself.

DE GUICHE: *(angrily)*
> My chair — my porters — I'm leaving.
> *(turning to CYRANO)*
>
> And as for you —

VOICE: *(offstage)*
> The chair of Monseigneur le Comte de Guiche!

DE GUICHE: *(regaining his composure)*
> Do you know Cervantes' 'Don Quixote'?

CYRANO:
> As if he were myself.

DE GUICHE:
> You should re-read —

A PORTER: *(at the door)*
> Your chair awaits!

DE GUICHE:
> —the chapter on the windmills.

CYRANO: *(pedantically)*
> Chapter thirteen.

DE GUICHE: If you're fool enough to fight with windmills,
> They may swing around and pitch you firmly
> In the mud.

CYRANO:
> Or up into the stars.

(DE GUICHE exits and, through the window, is seen climbing into his chair. The CADETS murmur among themselves. The CROWD thins out and wanders off.)

LE BRET: *(exasperated)*
> Now you've done it. Now you've really done it.

CYRANO:
> There's that sound again: Le Bret scolding.

LE BRET:
>   You must admit — destroying every chance
>   Is somewhat excessive.

CYRANO:
>   Very well then,
>   I admit I'm 'somewhat excessive'.

LE BRET: *(triumphantly)*
>   You do!?

CYRANO:
>   But certain things there are within this world
>   That *should* be carried to excess.

LE BRET:
>   If only
>   You'd forsake your foolish sense of honor
>   And of glory —

CYRANO:
>   What then should I do?
>   Find myself an accommodating patron
>   And like a sickly clinging vine crawl 'round
>   His trunk because I cannot stand alone?
>   No, thank you, no. Scribble fulsome
>   Odes to helpful bankers? Or play the fool
>   And try to raise a smile upon the lips
>   Of some officious politician? — No! —
>   Eat toads for breakfeast every livelong day?
>   Bruise my knees and undulate my spine
>   By grov'lling in the dust for charity?
>   No, thank you, no. — Or scratch the back
>   Of some scoundrel in the hope that he,
>   The favor done, might scratch mine in return.
>   Have my right hand scrounge for filthy lucre
>   While my left pretends it knows him not?
>   Take the Promethean fire that God gave me
>   And use it to burn incense at the altar
>   Of some measly little idol made
>   Of wood? — No, a thousand times no!
>   Become the biggest fish in some small pond
>   (Or, better still, to switch the metaphor)
>   Navigate my boat with madrigals
>   For oars, my sails billowing with the sighs

Of superannuated ladies? — Never!
Publish verses at my own expense
And make my vanity my muse? No thanks.
Be the guru of a fervent clique
Of pretentious scribblers that convene
Each Tuesday night for gossip and for dinner?
No, thank you, no. No and no again!
Shall I be like those who base their talent
On a single poem then never deign
To write another? Or carry on like those
Whose only joy is savouring the trite
And arid pleasures of the commonplace?
Whose only goal's to infiltrate their name
Within the columns of 'Mercure Francaise'.
I thank you, no. That's not a goal for me.
To calculate, ingratiate and fawn.
Make a gesture rather than a poem.
Seek favors, mentions, useful introductions!
No, thank you, no. I thank you all
Again, but no! —
            But to sing, to laugh
To dream, to go my own way by myself
And glory in my singularity,
To see things lucidly for what they are,
To wear my crumpled hat the wrong-way-round,
If I so choose. To fight for this or that,
A 'Yes' a 'No' — whatever takes my fancy.
To stroll beneath the sun or stars or moon
And take whatever turning that I please.
To never write a line that did not spring
From my own heart and mind. And modestly
Declare to one and all: — "I'm well content
With flowers, fruits and even weeds, so long
As they are gathered in a garden that
One can call one's own." — And if I gain
Some small success, to render Caesar nothing!
In short, to never be a parasite.
And if Nature, in her wisdom, makes me
Not as mighty as a towering oak
Or majestic as a mountain pine,

I'll grow where I am planted. Though not tall,
At least alone.
LE BRET:
     Alone, yes, but why
One against the world? What perverse streak
Is it that turns most everyone you meet
Into an enemy?
CYRANO:
     Perhaps the sight
Of others making friends — as dogs do in
The park. — sniffing out their courtesies.
My friends, I hope, are of a different breed,
And so it is with some relief I cry:
"Thank God, here comes another enemy."
LE BRET:
This is sheer madness.
CYRANO:
     A foible, nothing more.
To displease gives me pleasure. And I feed
On enmity. — Imagine how it feels
To walk beneath the silent thunder of
A thousand angry eyes — with specks of bile
And wads of angry spittle splattering
One's tunic as one goes. — You who worship
At the shrine of popularity
Are like the men who wear those great Italian
Collars, loose and free, in which one's neck
Is deep-submerged in flowing folds of silk.
While I, constrained within a stiff and Spanish
Ruff — as if be'ringed by enemies
At the throat — must hold myself erect
And wear the hatred of the common herd
Both as a millstone and a halo.
LE BRET: *(after a pause, placing his arm through CYRANO's)*
       Yes…
Be proud and stern to all the world, but then
Turn to me and say, she loves thee not.
CYRANO: *(sharply)*
Hush.

(A moment before, CHRISTIAN has entered, tried to socialize with the CADETS and has been silently rebuffed. He retires to a small table where LISE waits on him.)

CADET: *(Rises at his table, glass in hand.)*
Cyrano, — your story!
CYRANO:
                              — All in good time.

(On LE BRET's arm and talking in undertones.)

CADET: *(Coming forward)*
The story of the fight. — It will be
A fitting object-lesson for this…
(approaching CHRISTIAN)
                              brainless
Know-nothing.
CHRISTIAN:
                    Do you speak to me?
2ND CADET:
Yes you, you Northern jellyfish.
CHRISTIAN:
                              Sir!
1ST CADET:
Now listen close, M'sieur de Neuvillete:
There is one subject here that is forbidden
And which, no matter what, must never be
Alluded to.
CHRISTIAN:
            Really? And that is…?
1ST CADET: *(ominously)*
Watch me closely…
(He slowly taps his finger to his nose three times.)
                              Do you understand?
CHRISTIAN:
You mean the no —
3RD CADET:
                    — That word's not to be uttered!
(gesturing towards CYRANO)
To do so means you'll have to deal with him.

2ND CADET: *(who has slinked over towards CHRISTIAN)*
    Once he even slayed a man for simply
    (nasally)
    Talking through his nose.
4TH CADET: *(also in close proximity to CHRISTIAN)*
                        Any passing
    Reference, no matter how oblique,
    Or vague, and you will wake to find yourself
    Six feet underground.
5TH CADET:
                    A word…
1ST CADET:
                            A hint…
2ND CADET:
    A sign…
3RD CADET:
            …a gesture
4TH CADET:
                        or, God forbid, a sneeze,
1ST CADET:
    And your handkerchief becomes your shroud.

(There is a tremulous silence as all the CADETS surrounding CHRISTIAN glare ominously at him. After a moment, he rises and approaches CARBON DE CASTEL-JALOUX.)

CHRISTIAN:
    Captain.
CARBON:
            Sir.
CHRISTIAN:
                    Perhaps you can inform me:
    What is the proper course of action when
    Gascons become too cocky.
CARBON: *(surveys the CADETS and CHRISTIAN, weighing up the situation)*
                        Why to show them
    A Norman is as proud a man as they. *(turns back to his business)*

(CHRISTIAN digests the information and returns to his table.)

1ST CADET: *(to CYRANO)*
Come now, the story!

(The CADETS, improvising comments and exhortations, urge CYRANO to begin. They form an attentive group around him and sit in anticipation of the story. CHRISTIAN, apart, straddles his chair. Eventually, the expectant murmur subsides and CYRANO, with a strong sense of occasion, begins.)

CYRANO:
I went alone to seek the blackguards out.
The moon above was like a silver watch
And then, as if that watch were thrust into
A pocket, it all went dark and not a cloud
Was in the sky. No lamps upon the streets.
So dark, you couldn't see beyond —
CHRISTIAN: —your nose?

(An electric pause as everyone looks to CHRISTIAN then back to CYRANO who slowly turns towards CHRISTIAN.)

CYRANO: *(quietly)*
Who is that man there?
1ST CADET:
                                — The new recruit.
He arrived this morning.
CYRANO:
This morning, you say?
CARBON: *(softly)*
                                His name is Christian de Neuvil—
CYRANO: *(realizing)*
                                                        Oh yes!
(By turns, his face turns white then red. He is almost set to pounce on CHRISTIAN when, with a superhuman effort, he suppresses his anger and resolves to continue as calmly as he can.)
As I was saying, it grew dark, quite dark.
You couldn't see your hand before your eyes.
And I was thinking, for the sake of one
Poor drunkard, I was going to offend
A mighty prince by sticking in my...

CHRISTIAN:

> …nose.

CYRANO:

> Oar! — sticking in my *oar* where it
> Did not belong. — And in doing so,
> I might have to pay…

CHRISTIAN:

> …through the nose.

CYRANO:

> The piper! — Pay the *piper*! — So I drew close,
> So close in fact that we were…

CHRISTIAN:

> Nose to nose!?

CYRANO: *Eye to eye!* — And since I'd come this far
> I had to see it through. Then suddenly,
> A blade flashed in the darkness so I climbed
> A fountain and I quickly took a—

CHRISTIAN:

> nosedive?

CYRANO:

> A *leap* across the bridge! — To no avail
> For in a moment there were dozens more;
> So close in fact, that we were…

CHRISTIAN:

> … rubbing noses?

CYRANO:

> *Hand to hand!* With fifty more approaching.
> I countered one and handed him…

CHRISTIAN:

> — a nosegay?

CYRANO: (*Leaps at* CHRISTIAN *confronting him directly. The others scramble over to get a better view.* CHRISTIAN *has not stirred;* CYRANO, *breathing heavily, tries again to master his emotions as he forces himself to continue.*)
> A *slash across the skull!* He dropped at once.
> The others all fell back upon their…

CHRISTIAN:

> — noses?

CYRANO:

> *Heels.* I skewered two, disarmed a third

And as another lunged, I left their leader
Wailing loudly with a…
CHRISTIAN:

> …bloody nose?

CYRANO: *(exploding)*
Out, I say! All of you!!!

(The CADETS make a mad dash for the door.)

1ST CADET:

> At last,

The tiger stalks his prey.
CYRANO: *(bellowing)*

> Out at once!

Leave us two alone!

(As the CADETS scramble to the Exit, we hear a flurry of the following lines.)

2ND CADET:

> He'll slice him up

Into little pieces.
RAGUENEAU:

> Into mincemeat?

3RD CADET:
You can use him in your pies.
RAGUENEAU:

> I'm white

As a sheet thinking about it.
CARBON:

> Out!

4TH CADET:
There'll hardly be enough to bury.
4TH CADET:

> It's ghastly.

(They void the room — some from the rear, some from the sides, others from the stairway. In a moment, they have disappeared and CYRANO and CHRISTIAN stand facing one another.)

(Slowly CYRANO moves a few paces to CHRISTIAN who stands immobile, then in a sudden and unexpected movement, he throws his arms around the befuddled Cadet.)

CYRANO:
You're brave, and that's a rousing sight to see.

(CHRISTIAN still stands dumbfounded.)

Don't you understand — I'm her brother.
CHRISTIAN:
Whose?
CYRANO:
Hers.
CHRISTIAN:
Hers — Who?
CYRANO:
Roxane.
CHRISTIAN:
You, her brother?
CYRANO:
Practically. — More like
A cousin perhaps, than a brother.
CHRISTIAN:
She's told you?
CYRANO:
Everything.
CHRISTIAN:
That she loves me?
CYRANO:
What else?
CHRISTIAN: *(returning the embrace)*
M'sieur, I cannot tell you how happy I am.
CYRANO:
A sudden transformation.
CHRISTIAN:
Please, forgive me.
CYRANO: *(inspecting him from a distance)*
True, you're not such a bad-looking fellow.

CHRISTIAN:
If you only knew how much I admired you!
CYRANO:
And all those 'noses' —?
CHRISTIAN:
I apologize.
I do. — I apologize profusely.
CYRANO: *(deliberately changing the subject)*
Roxane expects a letter.
CHRISTIAN:
What, from me?
CYRANO:
Whom else?
CHRISTIAN: *(perturbed)*
Oh no, that cannot be.
CYRANO:
Pardon?
CHRISTIAN:
A letter from me — that cannot be?
CYRANO:
Why not?
CHRISTIAN:
If I were to write, I'd spoil it all.
CYRANO:
How so?
CHRISTIAN:
Because…because…I am so stupid that I'd —
I'd simply die of shame.
CYRANO:
A moment ago
You were not particularly stupid.
Irritating perhaps, — but not stupid.
CHRISTIAN:
To pick a quarrel, there's no art in that.
I can hold my own like any soldier.
But with a woman I am paralyzed.
Speechless. Mute. I look at them; their eyes
Smile fondly back at me…
CYRANO:
And not their hearts?

CHRISTIAN:

    No — for I know it well and tremble

    At the thought: I simply haven't got

    The knack to speak of love.

CYRANO:

                        How strange. Had I

    Been fashioned somewhat other than I am,

    I feel I could have done it with the best.

CHRISTIAN:

    Oh, if only I could find the words

    (hand to heart)

    To speak these thoughts.

CYRANO:

                     And if only I

    Myself were born a handsome Musketeer.

CHRISTIAN:

    And Roxane is highly educated.

    A few small words from me and I'd destroy

    All of her illusions.

CYRANO: Would *my* soul

    Find so handsome an interpreter!

CHRISTIAN: *(crestfallen)*

    How I wish I had but half your wit.

CYRANO: *(an idea dawning)*

    And so you shall — I'll lend it you — and in

    Return shall borrow your good looks. And out

    Of both we'll fashion one romantic hero.

CHRISTIAN:

    What?

CYRANO:

           I shall conjure up the words

    And you, my friend, shall speak them.

CHRISTIAN:

                      Do you mean—?

CYRANO:

    I mean she will not lose those fair illusions.

    What do you say? We'll win her both together?

    I'll take the heart that beats within this jerkin

    And breathe its words inside your fancy doublet.

CHRISTIAN:
> But Cyrano —

CYRANO:
>   Why not?

CHRISTIAN:
>   You frighten me.

CYRANO:
> I know: afraid you'll lose her altogether
> When the words are gone and all she has
> Is you. — But it's you yourself she loves.
> It may be my *words* upon your lips,
> But *your* lips that will win her in the end.

CHRISTIAN:
> Your eyes are blazing —

CYRANO:
>   Will you? Tell me, will you?

CHRISTIAN:
> Why should it mean so much to you?

CYRANO: *(elated)*
>   Because...
> *(catches himself, and adopts a carefree tone)*
> Because it is amusing — a kind of play.
> And what's more, appeals to my poetic
> Temperament. — A collaboration,
> If you like. I shall be your prompter
> Lurking in the darkness; you, the hero
> In the center of the stage who woos
> The lovely lady.

CHRISTIAN:
>   But then, there is the letter!
> I could never write it.

CYRANO: *(whipping out his letter to ROXANE from under his doublet)*
>   Voila, the letter!

CHRISTIAN:
> What's this?

CYRANO:
>   It only needs your signature.

CHRISTIAN:
> But —

CYRANO:

        I assure you it will do the trick.

CHRISTIAN:

    I don't understand. — How can you have —?

CYRANO:

    Poets always have a stash of letters
    To Chloris — Phyllis — Juliet — or Jane.
    It's stock-in-trade. For when we rhapsodize,
    Any pretty little name will serve the turn.
    Take it, and bring my airy fancy down
    To earth. — For these pleadings, pangs and painful
    Protestations, being insincere,
    Will be much more eloquent than truth.

CHRISTIAN:

    But won't I have to change a sentence here
    Or there? To make it fit Roxane?

CYRANO:

                        It fits,
    I assure you, as if 't'were made especially
    For her.

(CHRISTIAN looks at CYRANO for a moment then in a spasm of gratitude, throws himself into his arms.)

CHRISTIAN:

    —How can I ever thank you?

(Upstage, a CADET stealthily creeps in.)

CADET:

    Silent as the grave. I daren't look.

(Peeps his head in as tentatively, the other CADETS also enter. They encounter CHRISTIAN in CYRANO's arms, the two men fondly embracing. — They are dumbstruck. A general murmur of disbelief ripples through the group.)

CARBON:

    Our devil, it appears, has been converted.
    Not only has he turned the other cheek,

His nose, it seems, has turned around as well.

(The MUSKETEER with the large handlebar moustache, approaches, brazenly.)

MUSKETEER:
The ban is lifted. — Now anyone who wants
Can talk about his nose.
(calling out)
                              Lise, come out!

(LISE emerges as the MUSKETEER, even more emboldened, begins to mock CYRANO at close quarters.)

Sniff-sniff — what's that smell that's in the air?
Like something rotten and gone bad.
(holding his nose)
                              Pyoo.
(to CYRANO)
Surely m'sieur, you can smell it too!
(playfully)
I wonder what that smell can be?

CYRANO: *(sniffing exaggeratedly, approaches the MUSKETEER, sniffs his way over to his handlebar moustache, takes it into his two fingers and pretending to have uncovered the smell, announces)*
                              Stinkweed!

(CYRANO elbows the MUSKETEER in the belly causing him to double-over then gives him a kick which knocks him flat on his back. The CADETS, realizing that CYRANO is himself again, whoop for joy and do cartwheels as the CURTAIN falls.)

Act III

ROXANE'S KISS

A small square in the old Marais. Behind, a huddle of old houses and narrow winding streets. On the Right, ROXANE's house and a garden wall overrun with shrubbery. Above the door, a balcony and high window; beside it, a bench. The wall is threaded with clinging ivy; jasmine clings to the balcony and hangs quivering beneath. Using the bench and the stones jutting from the wall, it would be quite easy to climb to the balcony. On the opposite side, a similar old house, also made of brick and stone. Its entrance door has a large knocker wrapped in linen like a stubbed thumb. At rise, The DUENNA is seated on the bench beside the door. The window leading to ROXANE's balcony stands open. RAGUENEAU, dressed in a kind of livery, stands beside her. As he tells his mournful tale, he frequently pats his eyes with a damp handkerchief.

RAGUENEAU:
    And so she left me for a Musketeer.
    I was shattered — alone — nothing to do
    But hang myself — which I did.
    (pats his eyes while the DUENNA waits intently for him to continue)
                        And then,
    M'sieur de Bergerac came by and cut
    Me down and offered me this job as steward
    To his cousin.
DUENNA:
                How could you have fallen
    Quite so low?
RAGUENEAU:
              Lise loved the soldiers,
    I, the poets. Mars wolfed down the pastry
    I left out for Apollo. — And before long,
    It all came tumbling down around my ears.
DUENNA: *(rises and calls up to the balcony)*
    Roxane, are you ready? They're waiting for us.
ROXANE: *(from inside)*
    Just putting on my cloak —
DUENNA: *(gesturing to the house opposite)*
                  Clomire, you know,

Holds her salon every other Thursday.
All the brightest wits assemble there.
This afternoon there'll be a dissertation
On the Tender Passion.
RAGUENEAU:

                  The Tender *Passion?*
DUENNA: *(lyrically)*
The *Tender* Passion.
RAGUENEAU: *(corrected)*

              Ah, The *Tender* Passion.
DUENNA:
Hurry Roxane, we mustn't keep 'The Tender
Passion' waiting.
ROXANE:

              I'm coming in a moment.

(We hear the sound of stringed instruments approaching and CYRANO's voice la-la'ing in the distance.)

DUENNA: *(surprised)*
Listen, someone's serenading us.
CYRANO: *(enters followed by two pages carrying lutes.)*
That's supposed to be 'legato', sot.
1ST MUSICIAN:
I played 'legato' sir, if you were listening!
CYRANO:
You dare to argue with a pupil of
The Great Gassendi? — You wouldn't know a 'legato'
From a 'potahto', here, give it here!
(CYRANO plucks the lute away and finishes the phrase himself.)
ROXANE: *(on the balcony)*
Cyrano, is that you?
CYRANO: *(segueing the song into his reply)*

                Yes, tis I.
Serenading all your lilies-fair
And your roses-red.
ROXANE:

             —Wait for me,
I'm coming down.
(disappears)

DUENNA:

All these virtuosi?

Are they yours?

CYRANO:

I won them on a bet
With D'Assoucy. We differed on a point
Of grammar. Suddenly, he clapped his hand,
Pointed to these cooing nightingales
And said: "If I'm wrong I'll give them you
For one full day to play what'er you will!"
He lost of course, and so until tomorrow
Noon, they are my private virtuosi
To do with as I please. — I must admit
Their harmonies begin to pall. —
(turns to his musicians)

Enough!

Go play a grave pavanne for Montfleury
And tell the pig the music is on me.

(The Musicians, sulkily make for the exit as CYRANO *turns to the*
DUENNA.*)*

I come to inquire as I usually do —
(afterthought to his musicians as they are leaving)
— And make sure it's out of tune, you hear!
(back to the DUENNA*)*
— Whether she's still taken with her soulful
Admirer.

ROXANE: *(entering on the last)*

As brilliant as he's fair;
I love him even more.

CYRANO:

His intellect

As well?

ROXANE:

A mind as brilliant as your own.

CYRANO:

Well then, I'm impressed.

ROXANE:

I've never heard

A man express 'sweet nothings' which are still
So pregnant and so rich. Sometimes, there is
A lapse — his inspiration flags — and then
He rallies with a brilliant metaphor.
CYRANO: *(skeptical)*
    Well, good for him.
ROXANE:
                    How cynical you are!
You think a handsome man can have no brains!
CYRANO:
    He speaks well then, in matters of the heart?
ROXANE:
    More than 'speaks'; he *looses* poetry.
CYRANO:
    And writes as well?
ROXANE:
                Better than he speaks.
    Listen to this:
    (reciting by rote)
    "The more I lose my heart
    To you, the more of it I have."
    (admirously)
                      Well!?
CYRANO:
    A bit banal.
ROXANE:
    Or this: — "If in giving
    All my heart to thee, I then should lose
    My own, why then, prithee, send me yours!"
CYRANO:
    First he has too much heart and then
    He asks for yours. Can't he make up his mind!?
ROXANE:
    Oh you're insufferable — and you're jealous —
CYRANO: *(with a start)*
    Jealous!
ROXANE:
           Of his talent. Poets are all
    Like that. You must admit his closing lines
    Are the very tenderest thoughts of all.

"Though my fingertips relay my kisses,
I pray that you receive them with your lips."
CYRANO:
    A bit much, don't you think? *Un peu de trop.*
ROXANE:
    And there's this one —
CYRANO:
                Do you know them all
    By heart?
ROXANE:
          Every single one.
CYRANO: *(twisting his moustache)*
              Flattering,
    Very flattering.
ROXANE:
           He's a master-craftsman.
CYRANO:
    A dazzling wit, I must concede.
DUENNA:
                Quick,
    M'sieur de Guiche is coming.
    (pushing CYRANO off)
                    Get inside!
    If he finds you here, he may suspect.
ROXANE: He's still enamored and I fear his spite
    May work against us both. — A glance from him
    Would wither all my roses!
CYRANO: *(entering the house)*
             Very well.
ROXANE: *(as DE GUICHE enters)*
    We were just leaving.
DE GUICHE:
           I've come to say goodbye.
ROXANE:
    You're leaving Paris?
DE GUICHE:
           On orders! — To the war zone.
ROXANE:
    The war?

DE GUICHE:

> Tonight. We march to Arras where
> We are ordered to invade.

ROXANE: *(preoccupied)*

> Arras.

DE GUICHE:

> It seems the news does not arouse concern.

ROXANE:

> It does, it's only that —

DE GUICHE:

> As for myself
> I must confess it's like a mortal blow.
> I've no idea when we shall meet again.
> You may have heard that I've been made commander.

ROXANE: *(indifferent)*

> Bravo.

DE GUICHE:

> Of the regiment of the Guards.

ROXANE: *(startled)*

> The Guards? They're leaving?

DE GUICHE:

> Under my command.
> Including your cousin, that loud, pretentious braggart.
> I can't wait. — Revenge is sweet they say.

ROXANE: *(changing color)*

> Are you sure? The Regiment of the Guards?

DE GUICHE:

> I have the order here. No question about it.

ROXANE: *(aside)*

> Oh Christian, no.

DE GUICHE:

> — What is the matter, madame?

ROXANE: *(forcing herself to recover)*

> Off to battle — p'rhaps never to return —
> It is not easy when a woman cares.

DE GUICHE: *(his hopes raised)*

> You say this now — to me — the very moment
> That I — ?

ROXANE: *(abruptly changing her tone)*

> So, you would take revenge

93

Against my cousin, Cyrano? Would you truly?
DE GUICHE:
    Are you so very close?
ROXANE:
                  I hardly see him.
DE GUICHE:
    I, alas, see far too much of him,
    And always in the company of that
    New recruit — de Neuv — Villen — Viller —
    Whatever his name is!
ROXANE:
              A tallish fellow.
DE GUICHE:
    Blond.
ROXANE:
      Rosy cheeks?
DE GUICHE:
           Good looking —
ROXANE:
                  Hmm —
DE GUICHE:
    But a fool.
ROXANE:
      — Or so he may appear.
    (switching subject abruptly)
    Just now, you said that you would be revenged
    On Cyrano. But facing all the dangers
    Of a battle only brings him joy.
    If I were of your mind I know what I
    Would do!
DE GUICHE:
      And what is that?
ROXANE:
                Leave him behind
    To cool his heels in Paris while his comrades
    Show their valor on the battlefield.
    Why, that would be insufferable to him.
    It would wound his ego, which is where
    A man like him is mainly vulnerable.

DE GUICHE: *(after a beat)*
    Who but a woman could devise a plan
    As sinister as that?
ROXANE:
                He would eat
    His heart out, and all his Gascon friends
    Would languish being left behind. And *then*
    You'd be avenged.
DE GUICHE: *(coming closer)*
             You do care for me,
    A little, don't you?
    (ROXANE smiles non-commitally)
               Or else you'd never make
    My enemies your own. — That is a sign
    Of true affection, is it not?
ROXANE:
             They say
    It is, and I'd not disagree.
DE GUICHE: *(revealing a pack of letters)*
            You see,
    These orders — one for every company —
    Save this — *(removes one)* which is intended for the
                      Guards.
    I shall see that this one's not delivered
    And Cyrano's thirst for battle, remain unquenched.
    (getting even closer to ROXANE)
    You have your little wiles, don't you?
ROXANE:
              Sometimes
DE GUICHE:
    You know I'm mad for you — you've always known.
    (now very close)
    Now listen: tonight I should be gone and yet
    When I feel you trembling here beside me —
    Listen: there is a little convent-hall,
    Beside the Rue d'Orleans; 'twas founded by
    A sect of Capuchins and none but they
    May ever enter there. But since their sleeves
    Are wide enough to cover even me,

I shall convey myself within those walls.
These monks attend my uncle Richelieu
And fearing him, they will oblige his nephew.
After everyone believes I've gone,
In this disguise I'll come to you and thus,
We'll savour our caprice alone, together.

ROXANE:
But if this should be revealed, just think —
Your reputation —?

DE GUICHE:
                Bah.

ROXANE:
                   Your duty, honor —

DE GUICHE:
Piffle. — Only say that you'll be there.

ROXANE: *(playacting)*
I mustn't.

DE GUICHE:
          I entreat you.

ROXANE:
                  — I should resist.

DE GUICHE:
You're weakening, I feel it.

ROXANE: *(pretends to succumb)*
                Please — go.

(aside)
I must get to Christian.
(to DE GUICHE, impetuously)
                  I would have you
Go forth proudly — steep yourself in glory.

DE GUICHE:
You do care then. — You can love.

ROXANE:
                  Only those
Whose safety I most fear.

DE GUICHE: *(enraptured)*
                I am transformed.

(kisses her hand)
Is that what you want?

ROXANE: *(admiringly)*
                Yes, my friend.

(DE GUICHE, transported, keeps his eyes fixed on ROXANE as she amorously returns his look. Then, buoyed up with her admiration, turns and goes.)

DUENNA: *(mocking ROXANE's tone)*
"Yes, my friend." — How wicked!

ROXANE:
                                        Don't you dare
To breathe a word to Cyrano! He'll think
I've robbed him of his battle.
(She turns towards the house and calls.)
Cousin, come!

(CYRANO re-emerges from the house. ROXANE points to the house opposite.)

ROXANE:
We're off to Clomire's house. To hear Alcandre
And Lymison.

DUENNA: *(putting her fingers in her ears)*
                        There are some things 'tis best
We do not hear at all.

CYRANO:
                        Don't mind me.

DUENNA: *(now at the house)*
Look, someone's bandaged up the knocker.
(addresses it)
Muted, I suppose, because you pound
Too loud and interrupt their eloquence.
(stealthily raises it then raps very softly)

ROXANE: *(as the door opens)*
Let's go in *(to CYRANO)* but when Christian comes
Ask him to wait.

CYRANO:
                        And what will you discuss
With him today. You always know beforehand.

ROXANE:
Today?

CYRANO:
                Well?

ROXANE:
>   You won't tell him, will you?

CYRANO: *(finger to lips)*
    Silent as the grave.

ROXANE:
>   We'll talk of nothing.
Or everything. I'll say: "Be free as the wind!
Improvise! Lyricize! Astonish me!"

CYRANO: *(smiling to himself)*
    Good.

ROXANE: *(finger to lips)*
         Not a word.

CYRANO: *(finger to lips)*
                   Not a word.

(She goes in — but almost immediately reappears.)

ROXANE:
He's always best when he's spontaneous.

CYRANO:
    Naturally.

(ROXANE again puts her finger to her lips and finally goes in.)

CYRANO: *(calling)*
         Christian!

(CHRISTIAN enters.)

>   — I now have your assignment.
Today, we may outdo ourselves. Come on,
No time to lose. — We must rehearse.

CHRISTIAN:
>   No.

CYRANO:
    No?

CHRISTIAN:
    — I want to wait here for Roxane.

CYRANO:
    What kind of madness is this? Come along!

CHRISTIAN:

    No, I'm sick and tired of all this!

    Taking all my words from you, my letters!

    Being like a player on the stage!

    It was all right at the start perhaps,

    But now she loves me. I must speak for myself.

CYRANO:

    Naturally.

CHRISTIAN:

             Why not? And who says that

    I can't? I'm not an idiot you know.

    It's not that I do not appreciate

    All I've learned from you. I do. But God,

    It's not so hard to take a woman in

    My arms and say —

    (ROXANE appears in the doorway, CHRISTIAN panics.)

             Don't go, Cyrano!

CYRANO: *(bows)*

    As you wish, my friend. Speak for yourself.

    (He goes.)

(ROXANE bids adieu to the members of the salon, naming them as they depart. "Barthenoide. Aleandre. Gremione.")

DUENNA: *(irked)*

    I *told* you we would miss 'The Tender Passion'.

(The guests depart in diverse directions. ROXANE sees CHRISTIAN, gives a highsign for the DUENNA to enter the house, leaving them alone, which she does.)

ROXANE:

    The air is balmy now and evening's falling.

    Everyone has finally gone. — Sit down.

    We shall be quite alone.

(They both sit on the bench. CHRISTIAN both amorous and nervous. ROXANE expectant.)

    You may begin.

(Involuntarily, CHRISTIAN looks over his shoulder for CYRANO then back to ROXANE.)

I'm listening, *(whispers)* begin.
CHRISTIAN: *(after a pause)*
                                        — I love you.
ROXANE: *(closing her eyes)*
    Yes, speak to me of love.
CHRISTIAN:
                                        — I love you.
ROXANE:
    That's the theme, — now elaborate…
CHRISTIAN:
    I love you —
ROXANE:
                        — yes, yes, yes —
CHRISTIAN:
                                        A lot.
ROXANE: *(opens her eyes)*
    Yes, of course, I know, and then…
CHRISTIAN:
                                        And then…
    I'd be so happy if…
ROXANE: *(eyes closed)*
                            Happy if…?
CHRISTIAN:
    If you loved me too, Roxane. You do
    Love me, do you not?
ROXANE: *(wincing)*
                                    I crave champagne
    And all I get is watered-down vermouth.
    (trying to restore the mood)
    Tell me *how* you love me.
CHRISTIAN:
                                    — Very much!
ROXANE:
    Articulate your deepest feelings.
    (closes eyes)

CHRISTIAN: *(after a pause)*

Your neck.

ROXANE: *(eyes open)*
My neck?

CHRISTIAN:

I'd love to kiss it. — May I?

ROXANE:
Kiss my neck?

CHRISTIAN:

I love you.

ROXANE:

Not again!
(ROXANE rises, CHRISTIAN tries to keep her beside him.)

CHRISTIAN:
Not again! I mean, I do not love you —

ROXANE:
That's a little better —

CHRISTIAN:

I worship you.

ROXANE:
Oh really!
(ROXANE rises and frees herself.)

CHRISTIAN:

I know I grow ridiculous.

ROXANE:
Which irritates me quite as much as if
You had grown ugly.

CHRISTIAN:

I — I — I —

ROXANE:
Collect your thoughts; be soft and eloquent,
As well I know that you can be.

CHRISTIAN:

—I love —

ROXANE: *(out of patience)*
You love me, yes. I've got that message clear.
Adieu.
(starts for the house)

CHRISTIAN:

No, wait! — What I meant to say is —

ROXANE:
>That you adore me, yes, I've heard that too.
>Now kindly let me pass. I've had enough
>*(she moves hurriedly through the door slamming it in his face)*

(CYRANO, applauding, reappears.)

CYRANO:
>Bravo, bravo! A marvellous performance!

CHRISTIAN: *(pathetically)*
>Help me!

CYRANO:
>   What's it got to do with me?

CHRISTIAN:
>I'll die unless she loves me as before.
>Tell me what to do — at once!

CYRANO:
>   Instant
>Transformation — that's asking quite a lot!

(The window of ROXANE's balcony is suddenly illuminated.)

CHRISTIAN: *(pointing)*
>Look! — She's in her room. — I'm perishing.

CYRANO:
>Do it quietly, will you?

CHRISTIAN:
>   Please, I beg you!

CYRANO: *(looking about, hatching an idea)*
>It's rather dark.

CHRISTIAN:
>   And ? — and ? AND?

CYRANO:
>You know you don't deserve it.

CHRISTIAN:
>   Please, please.

CYRANO:
>Stand over there beneath the balcony.
>I'll crouch here and tell you what to say.

CHRISTIAN:
>What if she hears — what if she —

CYRANO:

> Shh, be quiet!

(The PAGES with their instruments return. As the 1ST PAGE lets out his first note, CYRANO claps his hand over his mouth — then places a finger to his lips instructing him to speak softly.)

1ST PAGE:
We finished serenading Montfleury.
What now?
CYRANO:

> You — go down to the end of the street!

(to another)
You — to the end of the other. If anyone
Appears, begin to play!
1ST PAGE:

> Play what, maestro?

CYRANO:
A waltz if it's a woman, pavanne for a man.
2ND PAGE:
We have a vast selection of waltzes, maestro.
French, Viennese —
CYRANO: *(shoving them off)*

> Any old waltz. — Go!

(The PAGES scoot off in opposite directions. CYRANO turns to CHRISTIAN.)

Now, call her!
CHRISTIAN: *(beneath the balcony)*

> Roxane! Roxane!

CYRANO: *(throwing some pebbles at the window)*

> This will fetch her.

ROXANE: *(slightly opening the window)*
Who's there?

(CHRISTIAN, tongue-tied, looks towards CYRANO who exaggeratedly mouths the words: "Tis I. Christian!")

CHRISTIAN: *(jumping to)*

> Tis I, Christian.

(CYRANO exasperatedly shrugs his shoulders.)

ROXANE:

Who?

CHRISTIAN:

Christian.

ROXANE:
    Oh, you again.

CHRISTIAN:

I had to talk to you.

CYRANO: *(whispering in the shadows)*
    Keep your voice down.

ROXANE:

I think it's best you go.

    You've nothing to say to me.

CHRISTIAN:

But I do, I do.

ROXANE:
    I don't believe you love me any longer.

CHRISTIAN: *(haltingly repeating the words whispered to him by CYRANO)*
    But I love you even more. How cruel...
    To doubt a man whose love... increases... even
    With every loving moment of each hour.

ROXANE: *(about to close the window, she halts now pleased with what she hears)*
    What is it you say?

CHRISTIAN: *(throughout, CHRISTIAN's words, lagging a beat or two behind, are relayed by CYRANO)*

My love is cradled

    In my soul just like... a stubborn child...
    That will not quit its cot.

ROXANE:

Is it not best

    To smother such a child at birth?

CHRISTIAN:

I tried,

    But failed in the attempt, for this newborn...
    Is powerful... as Hercules.

ROXANE: *(aside)*

Better.

CHRISTIAN:
>So strong in fact, he smote those double serpents…
>Doubt… and… Pride.

ROXANE: *(leaning over the balcony)*
>But tell me why you speak so haltingly?
>As if your imagination went on crutches?

CYRANO: *(vexed)*
>This is impossible! — Here, move away!
>*(angrily shoves* CHRISTIAN *aside taking his place beneath the balcony)*

ROXANE:
>Why are your words so hesitant tonight?

CYRANO:
>For in this inky murk that now surrounds us,
>They fall and stumble as they find their way.

ROXANE:
>But my words have no trouble finding *you*.

CYRANO:
>Because the door of my heart's open wide
>And welcomes them as friends. But *my* poor words,
>Like heavy bees o'er-burdened with their honey,
>Struggle upward to your ears. — Yours fall
>Lightly to the ground; while mine ascend.

ROXANE:
>Yet not so slowly as they did before.

CYRANO:
>They've quickly learned the way despite the distance.

ROXANE:
>Am I so far above you now?

CYRANO:
>   So far
>That if you dared to drop a cruel word
>The weight of it would crush me like a stone.

ROXANE: *(turning)*
>Then I"ll come down…

CYRANO:
>   No!

ROXANE: *(pointing to the bench beneath the balcony)*
>   — Then come closer!
>Perch yourself upon the bench!

CYRANO: *(recoiling into the shadows)*
Oh, no!!
ROXANE:

"No?!" And prithee, why so great a 'No'?
CYRANO: *(struggling against his feelings)*

Let me luxuriate within these shadows
And speak to you alone, remote, unseen.
ROXANE:

Unseen?
CYRANO:
Enchantingly invisible.
As night encloses all within its shroud
Making things indefinite and vague,
You glimpse but the outline of my cloak
And I, the shimmer of your summer gown
As the waning moon reflects its whiteness.
You're all light and I, all shadow, and O
How to express just what this moment means —
If ever I was eloquent…
ROXANE:
You were.
CYRANO:

But yet it's only now that you can hear
The true voice that is deep within me.
ROXANE: How so?
CYRANO:

Until tonight I only spoke through…
ROXANE:
What?
CYRANO:

Through that sweet intoxication that…
(CHRISTIAN makes a gesture warning him to get hold of himself.)
that…
Issues from your eyes and floods the world.
But tonight indeed, I speak to you
As if I've never spoken words before.
ROXANE:

It's true your voice *is* strange…
CYRANO:
How could it not be?

Tonight, at last I've *found* my voice — my own —
At last I dare to be myself — to —
(*He is overcome by the power of his own emotions; halts, tries to recover himself.*)

Forgive me.
What was I saying? — O, everything's so new.
ROXANE:
So new?
CYRANO:
Revealed I mean, and yet, to have no fear
Of moving you to mockery or —
ROXANE:

Mockery?
CYRANO: (*struggling to extricate himself*)
Because — what right have I, or any man
To dare to seek your love. My heart has ever
Felt the need to hide what it desired.
I'd yearn to pluck a star from out of heaven
But fearing ridicule, would kneel instead
To pick a simple daisy from the field.
ROXANE:
Even simple daisies have their charm.
CYRANO:
Not tonight, no imagery for us!
ROXANE: (*after a beat*)
You have never talked like this before.
CYRANO:
Similes and metaphors and little
Pretty phrases — is that all there is?
Let's escape and breathe unscented air,
Not spend each precious moment sipping honey
Out of dainty ornamental cups.
We live and breathe and deeply thirst for life.
O, let us meet it boldly — head on — like waves
That burst against the shore.
ROXANE:

But poetry —
CYRANO:
Is just a silly game to ward off life!
I tell you: once, and only once, there comes

A chance to take life boldly in one's arms,
When happiness stands just within our reach.
If then we pause or fill the gap with words,
It's lost to us for all eternity.

ROXANE:

  If that is true, and such a moment came
To us, what would you say —

CYRANO:

        I'd shatter language
Scatter to the winds the empty husks
And let them fall to earth where'er they may.
No grammar; no form; no style; no syntax; no sense.
"I love you!" — "I'm lost!" — "I'm smothered!" —
       "I'm wild!" — "I'm mad!"
"I love you" — "I'm faint" — No, no, it's all too much!
Your name hangs in my memory like the tongue
Of a golden bell within a rusted belfry.
I tremble at the thought of you and then
Your name rings out: "Roxane," "Roxane," "Roxane,"
And everything you are is then remember'd.
Last year, it was upon the twelfth of May,
You walked out in the morning with your hair
Untied and blowing loose about your shoulders.
You know how one that stares into the sun
Will for a time see sunspots 'fore his eyes,
So for hours was I blinded by
The radiance of your hair upon your back.

ROXANE: *(softly)*

  Yes, that indeed is love…

CYRANO:

       That cruel tyrant
That enslaves with jealousy and desire
Enkindling love then turning it to madness,
And yet, shows no concern unto itself.
To give you joy, I'd forfeit all my own
And in return would only ask to hear
The echo of your laughter in a room;
To glimpse you as you passed along the square.
Just seeing you breeds virtue in my soul
And makes my manhood stronger than it was.

Do you begin to understand me now?
To feel my body yearning up towards yours
Through all this gloom. — Tonight I have the courage
To say these things and realize that you
Can hear them being spoken. — It's too much!
In my wildest dreams I never dreamt
That this could be! I never dared to hope!
Now could I happily render Death my life,
Since finally, I've lived it to the full.
And it is my voice — mine — my very own,
That makes you gently tremble there above me;
Sending little shivers down the length
Of this reverberating branch of jasmine.
(he kisses the spray of jasmine on the hanging branch above him)
ROXANE: *(quietly, choked with emotion)*
    I tremble, and weep, and love you and am yours.
    Drunk with the thought of you.
CYRANO:
                        Then *let* me die,
    Since I, and I alone, have mixed the brew
    That brought about this stupor. — And yet, there is
    But one thing more that I would ask —
CHRISTIAN: *(under the balcony)*
                            A kiss!
ROXANE: *(startled)*
    What?
CYRANO: *(enraged, to CHRISTIAN)*
       You!
ROXANE:
          — You asked me for...?
CYRANO:
    I meant, I mean. —
(angrily to CHRISTIAN)
                 — You are too rash!
CHRISTIAN:
    She's willing. Why not make the most of it?
CYRANO:
    Yes, I asked, but then I realized
    How foolishly I —

ROXANE:

                  Is that all you ask?

CYRANO:

    All? And yet much more than I deserve.
    But it was presumptuous and so
    You must refuse.

CHRISTIAN: *(pulling at* CYRANO's *sleeve)*

                  But why?!

CYRANO: *(sotto voce)*

                Be quiet, Christian!

ROXANE:

    What is it you say?

CYRANO: *(loudly)*

              "Be quiet, Christian"
    I scold myself, for having such rash thoughts!

(The musicians begin to play in the distance.)

(To CHRISTIAN*)*
Someone approaches —

*(*ROXANE *shuts her window.* CYRANO *listens intently. One lute is playing a waltz; the other, a pavanne.)*

            A waltz *and* a pavanne,
    What can that mean?

*(*CAPUCHIN MONK *enters carrying a lantern and craning at each door.)*

            Aha, a priest, I see.
(to the Priest)
    A disciple of Diogenes perhaps?

CAPUCHIN:

    I'm looking for the house of —

CHRISTIAN: *(to* CYRANO, *impatiently)*

                 Get rid of him!

CAPUCHIN:

    …of Magdeleine Robin.

CHRISTIAN: *(vexed)*

              What blasted timing!

CYRANO: *(pointing out the way)*
    To the right and just keep going straight.
CAPUCHIN:
    Thanks, my son, I'll remember you in my prayers.
CYRANO:
    And I in mine.
CHRISTIAN: *(fuming)*
               — And I in mine.
CAPUCHIN:
                         Good evening.

    (He exits.)
CHRISTIAN:
    Get me my kiss!
CYRANO:
             — I think not.
CHRISTIAN:
                   But why?
    Sooner or later —
CYRANO:
                 — because you're young and she
Is fair, your lips will find each other out.
I know it very well. *(to himself)* Since it must be,
I prefer that I shall play Pandarus.

    (ROXANE's window opens again, CHRISTIAN ducks under the balcony.)

ROXANE:
    Christian, are you there?
CHRISTIAN: *(unthinkingly)*
                  I am,
CYRANO: *(shoving him aside)*
                  I *am.*
ROXANE:
    We were speaking of…of…
CYRANO:
                  a kiss.
Why should it be so fearful to pronounce,
When we know the thing itself's so sweet.
We shouldn't dread what's there to give us pleasure.
And didn't you, just now, quite quickly pass

From mockery to sighs, from sighs to tears?
The path from tears to joy is very short,
The flicker of a second brings you there.
ROXANE:
    Hush.
CYRANO:
            — And when all is said and done
What is a kiss? A vow that's sworn by two
That needs no stamp to seal it; a binding pledge
That needs no witnesses to make it firm.
A rosy mark that dots the 'i' in loving.
A tender secret whispered to the lips
And not the ear. A moment stolen from
Infinity. — Honey sucked by bees. —
The gentle exhalation of a flower.
A chance to hear the tremor of a heartbeat
And know the precious taste that two souls make
When they're united into one.
ROXANE:
                    Shhh.
CYRANO:
As Buckingham adored the Queen of France
And she bestowed a kiss upon her courtier,
So like him, I have my silent longings,
And like him, I dare adore a queen.
Like him, I'm faithful —
ROXANE: — and beautiful as well.
CYRANO: *(jolted)*
Yes, that too, I had forgot.
ROXANE: *(yielding)*
                Then come,
Pluck the flower that you covet so.
CYRANO: *(after a beat)*
You heard her, go!
ROXANE:
            Your "tender secret"—
CYRANO:
                    Move!
ROXANE:
Your "moment of infinity" —

CYRANO:

                    Climb up!

CHRISTIAN: *(hesitating)*
    I'm not sure — perhaps I —

CYRANO: *(pushing him)*

                        — Climb, monkey!

(CHRISTIAN pushes himself forward, then using the bench, the branches and the stones, reaches the balustrade and leaps over. Once there, he takes ROXANE into her arms and kisses her ardently. Below, CYRANO shuts his eyes and, as if by osmosis, tries to receive some of the pleasure of CHRISTIAN's kiss.)

What a curious torture! — There I am
At the feast of love, a kind of Lazarus,
Picking up the crumbs. — Still I have something
In my heart I've never had before.
It's my words that she's tasting in his mouth.
My words that have captivated her.

(The lutes start up again.)

A waltz and a pavanne. The Monk returns.
Holloa!
(Muffles his voice as if from far away and then pretends that he has just arrived.)

ROXANE:

               What's that? Who's there?

CYRANO:

                         Tis I.

Is Christian there with you?

CHRISTIAN: *(surprised)*

                    Cyrano!

ROXANE:

    Good evening, cousin.

CYRANO:

                 And good evening to you.

ROXANE:

    I'll be right down.
    (She disappears into the house.)

CHRISTIAN: *(spying the Capuchin)*
                    Oh no, not him again!
CAPUCHIN: *(to CYRANO)*
     It's here, I'm sure, that Madeleine Robin
     Resides.
CYRANO:
                    Robin, I thought you said *Rolin*.
CAPUCHIN:
     No, Robin! Madeleine Robin!
ROXANE: *(appearing at the front door, followed by RAGUENEAU holding a lantern)*
     Does someone call for me?
CAPUCHIN: *(exasperated, hands it over)*
                         At last! — A letter.
     Some noble matter I suspect as it
     Was sent by one that is a lord —
ROXANE:
                              De Guiche!
CHRISTIAN:
     How does he dare !? —
ROXANE:
                         Because he does not know
     My heart is yours. He will though, soon enough
     (using RAGUENEAU's lantern to read by, she scans the letter and mouths the words to herself)
     "Mademoiselle, the regimental drums
     Are beating loudly as I write. My troops
     Have buckled up their armor and go forth.
     But I remain behind and will conceal
     Myself in this small convent where I wait
     Hungrily for us to meet again.
     I send this precious news by way of one
     Who's innocent of what this note contains.
     The memory of your smile as I took leave
     Still tantalizes every waking moment.
     Be all alone tonight when he, too bold,
     Arrives to crave your pardon and your love.
     (to the CAPUCHIN)
     Father, this letter here pertains to you.
     (They gather round as she pretends to read.)

114

I'll read it out. Give ear: "Mademoiselle,
We must obey the Cardinal's will and this
Is why I send to you a Capuchin,
Most knowing and discreet, to be the holy
Instrument that executes his will.
It is our wish that he performs at once
The sacred rite of *(turns the page)* holy matrimony.
Christian, in a secret ceremony,
Must, this night, become your wedded husband.
Although I know you may resist this deed
Be resigned, for what the Cardinal
Decrees must be. He sends his holy blessing
To which I add my own. Your very humble —
Etcetera —
CAPUCHIN:

          There, I said that it
Must be some holy errand and by God,
It is!
ROXANE: *(aside to CHRISTIAN)*
     Do you like the style?
CHRISTIAN: *(nodding towards the CAPUCHIN)*
                    Watch out!
ROXANE: *(suddenly grief-stricken)*
     O heavens no, it cannot be!
CAPUCHIN: *(raising his lantern to CYRANO)*
                And you
I take it are the man that —
CHRISTIAN: *(pushing forward)*
                 I'm the bridegroom

(The Capuchin turns his lantern towards CHRISTIAN, clocks his good looks and begins to have some doubts. ROXANE, no longer grief-stricken sees this, and intercedes immediately).

ROXANE: *(taking up the letter)*
     Post Script: And in my name convey
Six hundred golden pistoles to the convent."
CAPUCHIN:
     Oh what a noble lord! *(to ROXANE)* Resign thyself
To the Cardinal's will.

ROXANE: *(martyring herself)*
                    I am resigned!

(RAGUENEAU opens the doors of the house to the CAPUCHIN, CHRISTIAN gestures for him to enter and as ROXANE follows them both, she turns to CYRANO.)

If De Guiche arrives, keep him here.
He mustn't interfere with —
CYRANO:
                    I understand,
    (to the CAPUCHIN)
    The service, how long?
CAPUCHIN:
                    A quarter of an hour.
CYRANO: *(hurrying them into the house)*
    Proceed, proceed, I'll wait out here,
ROXANE: *(to CHRISTIAN)*
                    Hurry.

(CHRISTIAN, overwhelmed with his good fortune, tries to embrace ROXANE but she trundles him indoors.)

CYRANO:
    Now to keep the Comte de Guiche amused
    For a quarter of an hour.
    (Using the bench as a stepping-stone, he climbs up the wall towards the balcony. Puts one finger at his right temple, the other at his left and visibly concentrates.)
                    I have my theme.

(The musician begins to play a pavanne. CYRANO cocks his ear.)

A man...

(The lute plays an ominous tremolo.)

                    and I can just imagine who!
    (CYRANO, perched on the balcony, experiments with an overhanging branch, measures the distance between himself and the ground.)
    Just high enough. — Now I must carefully

Infiltrate the earthly atmosphere.

(DE GUICHE masked, groping his way toward the house, enters.)

DE GUICHE:
    This blasted mask! Where's that bloody Capuchin?
CYRANO:
    Of course, he mustn't recognize my voice!
    (He mimes waving a magic wand over himself.)
    Be reborn an *emigrè francaise!*
DE GUICHE:
    This looks like the house. *(fumbling with it)* This
                    damned mask!

(As DE GUICHE enters, CYRANO leaps from the balcony, still holding on to the branch, and lands between him and the door. He pretends to fall heavily as if from a great height, flattens himself out on the ground and remains motionless. DE GUICHE gives a start.)

What's that?

(The branch springs back; looking upward, DE GUICHE sees only the sky and is befuddled.)

Where did he come from?
CYRANO: *(in a thick French-English accent, the brim of his hat concealing his features)*
    Ze moon.
DE GUICHE:
    Ze what??
CYRANO:
    What eeze ze time?
DE GUICHE:
    Ey?
CYRANO:
    What day eez eet? What saison? Where am I?
DE GUICHE:
    My dear sir.
CYRANO:
    Like a bomb'eh — I have fallen like a bomb'eh — from ze moon.

DE GUICHE: *(impatiently)*
>Now look, m'sieur…

CYRANO: *(rising up and in a terrible voice)*
>I say — from zee moon!
>*(pointing upward with an erect finger)*

DE GUICHE: *(humoring him)*
>Very well, if you say so.
>*(aside)*
>Just my luck, a moonstruck loon.

CYRANO: *(threateningly)*
>I am not making zee metaphors, m'sieur.

DE GUICHE:
>Pardon?

CYRANO:
>It was p'raps, a hundred years ago — perhaps only
>A moment ago — time has lost all meaning. But I know
>I was up zair in zat saffron-colored ball, ze moon.

DE GUICHE:
>Of course, now if you'll excuse me…

CYRANO: *(barring the way)*
>Where am I, m'sieur? Tell me ze truth — I can bear
>it — I can bear anyseeng! Hold back nussing! In what part
>of ze globe have I, like a human meteorite, fallen to ze
>ground?

DE GUICHE: *(exasperated)*
>Bloody hell!

CYRANO: *(horrified and incredulous)*
>Non?

DE GUICHE: *(bristling with impatience)*
>Would you kindly…

CYRANO:
>I could not choose where I fell to earth — eet was all
>so queek. And I *must* know: is zis anozer planet?
>Anozer moon? To which new exterior has ze dead
>weight of my posterior brought me?

DE GUICHE:
>Sir, I tell you again…

CYRANO: *(recoiling from De Guiche's black mask)*
>Mon dieu! Ees it Afrique? — Are you a canny-bal??

DE GUICHE: *(involuntarily touching his mask)*
  This is a mask, m'sieur.
CYRANO:
  Are we in Venice? In Monte Carlo?
DE GUICHE: *(trying to pass)*
  I have a date with a lady, sir.
CYRANO: *(relieved)*
  Ah, Paree!
DE GUICHE: *(amused, in spite of himself)*
  The fool grows droll.
CYRANO:
  You smile.
DE GUICHE:
  I smile, but I still want to pass.
CYRANO:
  Ah cher Paree.
  (arranging his clothes and preening)
  Quelle bonne chance! — Excuse my appearance,
  I caught ze last thunderbolt leaving from Saturn
  and that ees ze worst transportation you can possibly
  get. It's very much ze long-way-round and ze ether, I
  am afraid, is still clinging to my clothes. My hair
  is feelthy wiz stardust and these white marks on my
  sleeve are splotches, not yet dried, from ze Milky
  Way; messy constellation that eet is!
  (Rubs imaginary marks off his sleeve.)
DE GUICHE: *(impatiently)*
  M'sieur.
CYRANO: *(as DE GUICHE tries to push past, he holds up his leg)*
  You see zees bite? — a nasty souvenir from ze Great
  Bear. And when I passed by Saturn I sought my ears
  would explode.
DE GUICHE:
  Your ears?
CYRANO:
  From ze *rings* you know; zey can be quite deafening.
  Ze Big Bear is just above Ze Big Dipper, and I don't
  know what zey have been scooping up in zat Dipper
  lately, but it smelt awful — and I have a nasty
  suspicion, ze Great Bear had somesing to do wiz zat.—

When I put all zees stories togezher in a book, it weel be
quite heavenly — no pun intended. Sank God I saved a
few of ze leetle stars on ze way down, as I am sure
zey'll come in handy as asterisks.

DE GUICHE:
That is quite enough, m'sieur.

CYRANO: *(brushing his clothes)*
More zan enough, if you ask me! — Would you like to
know ze nature of ze moon's surface, ze population, ze
climate?

DE GUICHE: *(losing his temper)*
I wish to know nothing about it!

CYRANO: *(rapid-fire)*
Of course, what you really want to know is how zid
I launch myself to ze moon in ze first place. Well
m'sieur, between you and I, it was an invention of my
own making!

DE GUICHE: *(aside)*
Just my luck, a hairbrained idiot.

CYRANO:
I scorned to use ze eagle of Regiomontanus or ze pigeon
of Archytas…

DE GUICHE:
A learned idiot!

*(De Guiche manages to push towards ROXANE's door but CYRANO again
bars the way.)*

CYRANO:
I invented not one, but seex ways to penetrate ze
heavens.

DE GUICHE: *(confused)*
Seex?

CYRANO:
I streep myself naked like ze day I was born,
attache crystal vials filled wiz morning dew to
every part of my body and, as the sun rises, I rise
wiz it — up into ze skies — vaporized into ze
stratosphere,

DE GUICHE:
> That's one.

CYRANO: *(barring his path again as DE GUICHE tries to maneuver forward)*
> Or, compressing ze air in a cedar chest and wiz
> ze use of mirrors and icosahedron, I create a whirlwind
> on whose tail I flew into ze realms above.

DE GUICHE: *(stealthily trying to pass him on his other side)*
> That's two!

(CYRANO again bars the way.)

CYRANO:
> Or by carefully feeting up a giant grasshopper fueled
> wiz pistons in ze front and saltpeter in za rear, I can
> vault upwards by leaps and bounds.

DE GUICHE: *(listening, in spite of himself but still edging forward)*
> That's three.

CYRANO: *(barring his path)*
> Or, since smoke has a natural tendency to rise, I pump
> eet into a transparent balloon, place myself inside and
> letting nature take eets course, merely gravitate
> on high.

DE GUICHE:
> Four!

(same business)

CYRANO:
> Or, since Diana, when her bow is at eets smallest,
> loves to suck up ze innards of bulls and goats, I anoint
> myself accordingly and so ascend.

DE GUICHE: *(still trying to edge forward but becoming mesmerized by him)*
> Five!

CYRANO: *(who has now diverted him across the street and over to the bench)*
> And ze *piece-de-resistance!* While seated on a plate
> of iron, I throw a magnet into ze air, get sucked up by
> ze iron, throw eet again, rise further still, and in zees
> way magnetize myself — throw by throw — until
> arriving at ze threshold of ze moon.

DE GUICHE:

Six! — And which of these ingenious methods did you
select?

CYRANO:

The seventh!

DE GUICHE:

And that was…?

CYRANO:

Can you guess?

DE GUICHE: *(aside)*

One can become addicted to this idiot!

CYRANO: *(imitating the sound of waves lapping on the beach and waving his arms in great, flying motions)*

Whoop — whoop — whoop — Have you guessed yet?

(DE GUICHE, mesmerized, watches the mime-show and mechanically nods 'no'.)

Why wiz ze tides! — At zust zat moment when
ze moon sucks up ze waves, I placed myself on
ze beach, having thoroughly immersed myself,
and wiz my hair steel dreeping wet, I slowly
gravitated upwards — like an angel celestially
ascending. — But just then — boom!

DE GUICHE: *(carried away in spite of himself)*

Boom??

CYRANO: *(in his own voice)*

Boom! The fifteen minutes are up, the couple
Bound in marriage and so, you may proceed.

DE GUICHE: *(suddenly recognizing the voice)*

That voice…

(The door of ROXANE's house opens and lackeys, holding lighted candelabra emerge. Light increases. CYRANO whips off his disguise and raises his nose aloft as if it were a triumphant banner.)

that nose… is it? is it?

CYRANO: *(bowing low)*

Cyrano, at your service. Yes, I believe
The marriage vows have been exchanged.

DE GUICHE:

The what?

(DE GUICHE turns quickly — just in time to see the newlyweds hand-in-hand, framed between the lackeys. The CAPUCHIN, looking very content, stands behind. RAGUENEAU holds a blazing torch to light the way. Bringing up the rear, The DUENNA dressed in a nightgown and still trying to assimilate the night's events. DE GUICHE incredulous, approaches ROXANE and CHRISTIAN.)

(to ROXANE)
You!
(turns to CHRISTIAN)
   Him?!

(The couple turn fondly to one another.)

CYRANO: *(in his phony accent)*
          And zon't forget me!
DE GUICHE: *(recovering, to ROXANE)*
   My compliments *(turns to CYRANO)* and to you as well,
   My loquacious traveller-in-space.
   Your stories would have hypnotized a saint
   And kept him from his date with Paradise.
   You shouldn't waste those fanciful ideas.
   You ought to write them down.
CYRANO: *(bowing)*
                I already have.
   It's called: "The Comic History of the Phases
   Of The Moon" — *(offering the book)* Twenty-two centimes.
   (presenting the bride and groom to DE GUICHE)
   The bridal pair that God, and you, have joined
   Together.
DE GUICHE: *(regarding them with cold fish-eyes)*
        So it would appear. — Madame,
   I fear you must now bid the groom adieu.
ROXANE:
   Adieu, but why—?
DE GUICHE:
          His regiment awaits him.

(to CHRISTIAN*)*
Report at once!
ROXANE:
                    You'd take him into battle?
DE GUICHE:
Why not? He is a soldier, after all.
ROXANE:
The Gascons are not summoned.
DE GUICHE:
                        They are now!
(brandishing the order from his pocket)
You will not disobey an order, sir!
ROXANE:
Christian!
DE GUICHE: *(looking at* CYRANO*)*
         The honeymoon must wait,
I fear.
CYRANO: *(aside)*
Somehow that news in no way puts me out.
CHRISTIAN: *(going for another kiss)*
Roxane!
CYRANO:
        Come, come, we can't be dallying
Forever.
CHRISTIAN:
       If you only knew how hard
It is to leave the woman that you love.
CYRANO: *(drawing him away)*
I have a little inkling I believe.

(The martial drums are heard in the distance.)

DE GUICHE: *(who has moved off)*
Come, the regiment awaits!
ROXANE: *(to* CYRANO, *still clinging to* CHRISTIAN*)*
                  I place him
Now within your care. O promise me,
That his life will never be in danger.
CYRANO: *(vexed, and urging* CHRISTIAN *out)*
I'll do the best I can — but after all —

ROXANE: *(still clinging to* CHRISTIAN*)*
    And see that he has everything he needs.
CYRANO: *(irritated, still dragging him away)*
    I'll try, I'll try.
ROXANE: *(still clinging)*
               Make sure he's warm, and see
    He never wants for food or drink.
CYRANO:
                      — Yes, yes.
ROXANE: *(urgently in his ear)*
    And is faithful to me always.
CYRANO: *(dragging* CHRISTIAN *away)*
                   Yes, of course.
ROXANE:
    And writes to me as often as he can.
CYRANO: *(stopping in his tracks)*
    Of that I can assure you! — Allons! Allons!
    *(*CYRANO *hauls* CHRISTIAN *out as the martial drums grow louder and the sound of marching feet swells in the background.)*

CURTAIN

Act IV

SOLDIERS OF GASCONY

The outpost at the siege of Arras occupied by CARBON DE CASTEL-JALOUX and his company. In the back, a rampart, the full length of the stage. Beyond it, a vast plain stretching out to the horizon. The walls of the city, roofs and other structures are silhouetted against the sky. Tents, diverse weapons, military drums, etc. In the east, a burgeoning yellow light marks the imminent dawn of day. Sentries, campfires. At Rise, we see several Cadets wrapped in their cloaks, asleep on the ground — CHRISTIAN among them. CARBON DE CASTEL-JALOUX and LE BRET, both looking thin and weary, are on guard. The group is lit by the flicker of bonfires. LE BRET grimly surveys the scene.

LE BRET:
    Awful.
CARBON:
        It is.
LE BRET:
                Positively frightful!
CARBON:
    Keep your voice down. — No point in waking them.
    (to the sleeping soldiers)
    Sleep.
    (to LE BRET)
        He who sleeps dines, they say.
    And those who sleep fitfully, dine on crumbs.
LE BRET:
    If only we *had* crumbs; that would be something.

(Sound of distant firing.)

CARBON:
    Damn those musketeers. They'll wake my babies.
    (To some of the soldiers roused by the gunfire.)
    Sleep on, sleep on.
    (The shooting comes closer. CARBON surveys the near distance.)
        Cyrano's coming back.

(The weary soldiers shuffle about and return to sleep.)

SENTRY: *(offstage)*
>Halt, who's there?

CYRANO: *(appearing on the parapet)*
>>>Bergerac, you idiot!

LE BRET:
>Thank God.

CYRANO: *(cautioning him to speak softly)*
>>Shh, be still.

LE BRET:
>>>>Are you wounded?

CYRANO:
>Their aim is always off just after sunrise.

LE BRET:
>Go on! Risk your life every morning
>Just to post a letter!

CYRANO: *(pausing beside the sleeping CHRISTIAN)*
>>>I said he'd write
>Once a day, and dammit, so he shall!
>*(looking down)*
>He's looking very pale and drawn and thin.
>But handsome none the less.

LE BRET:
>>>>>Get some sleep!

CYRANO:
>No more scolding. You know I'm very careful
>Whenever I cross the lines. It never fails,
>They are always drunk asleep.

LE BRET:
>>>>You should
>Have brought a little something back.

CYRANO:
>>>>>I can't.
>I have to travel light — but something tells me
>Tonight there'll be some news. The French will either
>Eat or perish.

LE BRET:
>>What do you mean?

CYRANO:
>>>>You'll see.

CARBON:
>The bold invaders going hungry, hmph!
>What a bloody way to wage a war?

LE BRET:
>We invade the Spanish and get caught
>In our own trap and now the Cardinal-Prince
>Of Spain turns round and fires down on us.
>It's bloody marvellous, isn't it!

CYRANO:
>Who knows ? Someone still may turn on him!

CARBON:
>It isn't funny.

LE BRET: *(shaking his head at* CYRANO*)*
>   And every single day
>You risk your life behind the lines to write a —
>Where're you going now?

CYRANO:
>— Another letter!

*(*CYRANO *enters the tent.)*

(A few more rays of daylight trickle in. The clouds take on a reddish hue. In the distance, a cannon shot is heard then a rumble of drums followed by a second rumble much closer. The drumbeats seem to be having a dialogue together. They grow louder then taper off and subside across the camp. A trumpet sounds. Gradually, everyone awakens; in the background, we hear the murmur of Officers' voices.)

CARBON: *(sighing)*
>Reveille again — another fractured
>Night of sleep. — And don't I know just what
>Their first words will be.

(The CADETS *gradually cast off sleep and begin to rouse themselves.)*

1ST CADET: *(yawning)*
>   O God, I'm hungry.

2ND CADET:
>My stomach's growling,

3RD CADET: *(squinting at the light)*
>   Not another day!

CARBON:
> Rise and shine!

1ST CADET:
> > I'd rather die in bed.

2ND CADET:
> I haven't got the strength to move a muscle.

1ST CADET: *(examining himself in his cuirass)*
> My tongue is like a melted piece of cheese.

3RD CADET:
> This climate isn't good for my complexion.

4TH CADET:
> I'd trade my barony for a loaf of bread.

2ND CADET:
> I've no stomach for this bloody war,
> And nothing in the stomach that I have.
> I think that I'll just stay inside my tent.
> Achilles did. What's good enough for him
> Is good enough for me.

5TH CADET:
> > A crust of bread,
> That's all I ask. A little crust of bread.

CARBON: *(aside to CYRANO in his tent)*
> Can't you lend a hand? You always raised
> Their spirits with a jest. They need it now.

2ND CADET: *(angrily, noticing the 1ST CADET chewing)*
> What are you eating there?

1ST CADET:
> > Axle-grease
> And cannon-wrapping! — Seems that they forgot
> To deliver pheasant here today.

6TH CADET: *(entering)*
> I've just been hunting in the woods.

7TH CADET: *(entering)*
> > And I've
> Been fishing in the Scarpe.

ALL: *(scrambling up towards them)*
> > What've you got?
> A carp? A chicken? A pheasant?

7TH CADET: *(holding it up)*
> > A gudgeon.

6TH CADET: *(holding it up)*

> And a sparrow.

(The men contemplate the meagre offerings and gradually well up with desperate cries of: 'Mutiny!' 'Revolt!' 'Enough' 'No more!' CARBON is frightened but holds his ground. With one hand on his saber, he turns to CYRANO pleadingly.)

CYRANO: *(Emerging from his tent, a pen in his ear, a book in his hand, regarding the CADETS who are slightly daunted by his composure. A troubled silence as the CADETS continue to regard him.)*
You there, what's the matter with your foot?
CADET:
There's something in my heel that aches.
CYRANO:

> What's that?

CADET:
My belly!
CYRANO:

> Strange, I've got the same complaint.

CADET:
Doesn't it get you down?
CYRANO:

> No, it makes me

Stand taller.
ANOTHER CADET:

> My teeth are getting rusty.

CYRANO:
Not in use? Then pull them out!
YET ANOTHER CADET:

> My belly's

Empty as a drum.
CYRANO:

> Try beating out

A rhythm on it. — *(goadingly)* Um, 'retreat' perhaps?
ANOTHER CADET:
I've got a nasty buzzing in my ears.
CYRANO:
The growling in your belly's even louder.
I can hear it from here.

YET ANOTHER CADET:
> O for a pint
> Of wine!

CYRANO: *(offering him his own helmet)*
> — You can use this as your flagon!

ANOTHER:
> If only there was something to digest!

CYRANO: *(throwing him his book)*
> Try the 'Iliad'!

ANOTHER:
> The politicians
> Eat four square meals a day.

CYRANO:
> Why not run
> For office? — Department of Fisheries perhaps.
> Then you'd have your sturgeon all year round.

ANOTHER:
> Why shouldn't I have Rhenish wine to drink?

CYRANO: *(pretending to talk as if to a servant)*
> "Ah Richelieu, do fill this fellow's goblet.
> It would appear his lordship has gone dry."

ANOTHER CADET: *(in agony)*
> O God, I am as hungry as a hog!

CYRANO:
> Then why not take a bite out of your head?
> Hog's-head's very tasty so they say.

1ST CADET: *(bitter)*
> Everything's a joke with you.

CYRANO:
> Precisely,
> The point of wit's to make a witty point.
> Any fool knows that — unless he's witless.
> If I'm to die, then let it be beneath
> A fading sunset with a jest upon
> My lips upon a subject worthy of
> The jest. Not in a bed but on a field
> Of honour — a length of steel lodged in my heart
> And on my quivering lips, a witticism
> That's every bit as pointed.

(The CADETS *spontaneously rise up against* CYRANO *wailing their hunger: "We're hungry!" "We want food — not jokes." "We're dying." etc.)*

Can't you think

Of anything except your bellies? Really!
(spying an old friend in the background)
Come Bertrandou, fifer, one-time shepherd.
Take your fife and play some ancient air
For these miserable malcontents.
Something warm and cozy redolent
Of home and country, and where every note,
As familiar as the face of loved ones,
Winds itself into our hearts the way
The curling smoke of chimneys after sunset
Used to float upon our village hills.
(The old man readies his fife.)
Let that warlike fife forget its wrath
And as your fingers ripple o'er its stops
Like some prancing little birds at play,
Recall that long before 'twas ever wrought
In ebony, it was a reed. And let it
Marvel at the music that it makes
Bringing back the memory of brooks,
Of forest-glades and gentle waterfalls,
When being like the saplings on the bough,
We never understood the paradise
Of being young.
(The old man begins playing an old Gascon melody.)
Listen well, my comrades, listen well.
Beneath his touch, it is no martial fife
But a shepherd's flute encountered in
The woods. It doesn't summon us to battle
But to watch the grazing sheep upon
The verge, the herdsman as he ambles by.
It is the vale, the moor, the rolling hills;
The sunburnt shepherd in his crimson cap;
The downy green of evening as it falls
On the Dordogne. It is the very soul
Of Gascony.

(CYRANO has indeed transformed the mood. The CADETS, glassy-eyed, peer into the middle distance, their heads low, their thoughts rooted in their homeland. One or two wipe away a tear upon their sleeve.)

CARBON: *(quietly to CYRANO)*
>There're tears in their eyes.

CYRANO:
Homesickness — a nobler malady
Than hunger; it reminds them that their hearts
Must also be fed.

CARBON:
>But it's not manly.

CYRANO: You think not?
(He gestures for the drummer to approach.)
>No teardrops can dissolve
The steel within their hearts. — Just watch —
(He gives a signal to the drummer who gives a loud martial roll on the drum causing THE CADETS to spring up immediately and go for their weapons with a great belligerent outcry.)
You see, what the piper lulled to sleep,
The martial drum awakens — in a trice!

A CADET: *(spying him up ahead)*
M'sieur De Guiche.

(The Cadets immediately growl out their displeasure.)

CYRANO:
>Not a flattering greeting.

2ND CADET:
He makes me sick.

3RD CADET:
>That collar made of lace…

4TH CADET:
And tucked around his armor…

5TH CADET:
>Like a ruffle
On a broadsword.

6TH CADET:
>A square of linen for a
Boil upon his neck.

133

7TH CADET:

                                Ever the Courtier!

1ST CADET:

  The scented nephew of the Cardinal.

CARBON:

  But still, he is a Gascon.

1ST CADET:

                                Not a true one!

  For look you here, all us Gascons are
  A little mad. Not him. He's as sane
  As sane can be. — Now you show me
  A reason'ble Gascon and I'll show you
  An impostor!

LE BRET:

                    He's looking very pale.

2ND CADET:

  He's as hungry as the next man here,
  But there's such a length of jewels around
  His waist, it makes his cramps look like they're sparkling
  In the sunlight.

CYRANO: *(quickly)*

  He's not to see us looking downcast. Quick.
  Out with the cards, the pipes, the dice…

(The CADETS proceed to busy themselves, light up, play dice, etc., as CYRANO whips out a small volume.)

                                          while I

  Commune with my Descartes.

DE GUICHE: *(to CARBON)*

                                Good morning.

CARBON: *(to DE GUICHE)*

                                          Good morning.

DE GUICHE: *(aside)*

  He's gone a sickly color.

CARBON: *(aside)*

                        He's all eyes.

DE GUICHE: *(surveying the CADETS coldly)*

  If looks could kill, as the saying goes
  I fear I'd be a dead man ten-times over.

I hear that I'm maligned on every side;
That haughty barons from Perigord and Bearn
Outdo each another to find an epithet
That suits their hated Colonel. 'Gutless courtier!'
'Scheming politician!' — and sneers because
My armor's draped with fine Italian lace.
It seems it is a great disgrace to be
A Gascon and yet not a ragged beggar!

(There is a brooding, sullen silence as the Cadets *continue, now in slow motion, to smoke and dice.)*

Shall I have your Captain punish such a
Show of insolent behavior?

Carbon:
                                        Not I.
I mete out no such punishment.

De Guiche:
        No?

Carbon:
                I pay my men. They belong to me.
As for proper, military orders,
Of course, I shall obey them.

De Guiche:
                                        That's quite enough!
(turns again to the Cadets*)*
I scorn your petty little intrigues and your
Cold disdain. — My conduct under fire
Is known throughout the field. And yesterday
At the battle of Bapaume, I routed
All the troops of Count de Bucuoi.
Charging thrice against all odds, myself
Leading every charge.

Cyrano: *(not looking up)*
                                And your white scarf?

De Guiche: *(his ego flattered)*
You heard of that then? — well, it's all quite true.
Rallying my troops for the third assault,
A sordid band of cowardly fugitives
Dragged me toward the enemy installation.

135

I stood in danger of being shot or worse,
Taken prisoner. But having my wits about me,
I took the silken scarf that marked my rank
And threw it off. Then, in the hurly-burly
That followed made my own way back to camp,
Rallied the troops, charged again and finally
Won the day. — Well, what d'you say to that?

(The CADETS, in spite of their indifference to DE GUICHE, have listened to his story with half an ear. Still turned away, their cards are held in check, their dice suspended, in their mouths, the smoke from their pipes not exhaled.)

CYRANO:
That Henry of Navarre, outnumbered and
Outgunned would never, in a million years,
Have abandoned his white plume.

(The CADETS silently exult in CYRANO's one-upmanship. The cards fall, the dice rolls, the smoke from their pipes billow out of their mouths.)

DE GUICHE:
                              Nevertheless,
The ploy achieved its end.
CYRANO:
                        Perhaps it did.
And yet, there is a certain privilege,
Nay an honor, that an officer
Enjoys in being such a noble target.

(The CADETS, again with cards, dice and pipes, express their satisfaction.)

Had I been there, (of course one man's sense
Of courage differs greatly from another),
When your scarf had fluttered to the ground,
I'd have scooped it up and put it on.
DE GUICHE:
Boasting, as usual.

CYRANO:

                 Boasting? Lend it to me
And I shall wear it 'round my neck tonight
As I lead the charge.

DE GUICHE:

                Empty arrogance!
You know quite well that scarf lies far behind
The enemy lines, upon a riverbank
That's pounded by artillery, and even
If a man could reach it, he would never
Venture back alive.

CYRANO: *(brandishing it from his pocket)*

                 Here it is!

(The CADETS suppress their gleeful laughter behind their cards and dice. DE GUICHE wheels around quickly to confront them; they immediately assume a false gravity and soberly proceed with their activities. One of them whistles the air the old fifer played recently; another hums the tune to himself.)

DE GUICHE: *(looking at his men and taking up the scarf)*

Thank you. This is just the bit of white
I needed to send a signal which till now
I'd hesitated to do. — Now I'll do it.

(He climbs up to the parapet and begins signalling with the scarf. The CADETS, immediately alarmed, begin to question one another: "What's he doing?" — "Who's he signalling?" — "What's it mean?")

SENTRY: *(on the parapet)*

There's a man down there. He's running off!

DE GUICHE: *(casually climbing down)*

A Spaniard and a double-spy. A man
Quite useful to our side, as he gives
The enemy the news that we would wish
For them to have and, in so doing, lets
Our troops anticipate their moves.

CYRANO:

                 A traitor,
In other words.

DE GUICHE: *(casually folding up his scarf)*
> But a useful one,
> And that's what counts. — What was I saying?—Yes.
> Here's some news you ought to know: Tonight,
> In one last effort to obtain supplies,
> The Marshall journeys to Dourlens alone.
> There he'll find the wagons filled with food.
> To make it back, he needs a mighty force.
> Half at least of all the men we have.
> A golden chance for Spaniards to attack
> Since we will be at only half our strength.

CARBON:
> But the Spaniards have no knowledge of
> The Marshal's plan.

DE GUICHE:
>   Alas, they do. In fact,
> We know they will attack.

CARBON:
>   — But how —

DE GUICHE: *(gesturing to where the Spaniard fled)*
>   Our spy.
> He came to warn me of their plans. And his
> Report will pinpoint where they strike.
> I told him: wander through the battle lines
> And where you see my signal being given,
> Let that be the point of their attack.

(The CADETS digest DE GUICHE's words then slowly turn to CARBON DE CASTEL-JALOUX.)

CARBON:
> Well gentleman!

(The CADETS rise, buckle on their breastplates and their swords.)

DE GUICHE:
> We have about an hour.

(The CADETS hearing that, shrug their shoulders and return to their cards and dice. "Ah well," says one. "No hurry then," says another.)

(to CARBON*)*
We must buy as much time as we can
For the Marshall.
CARBON:
                              And how do we do that?
DE GUICHE:
      By being so kind as to lay down all your lives.
CYRANO:
      And so you have your revenge!
DE GUICHE:
                              I do not harbor
      Any love for anyone of you.
      But after all, you are 'the bravest of
      The brave', France's 'gallant cavaliers',
      And I, the servant of my King and in
      His service, choose to sacrifice your lives.
CYRANO: *(saluting)*
      On behalf of all my men, I thank you.
DE GUICHE: *(returning the salute)*
      A hundred-to-one would appear to be
      Your favorite odds. You should be quite content.
      (He moves off with CARBON.*)*
CYRANO: *(looking his grim-faced soldiers squarely in the eye)*
      To our Gascon coat-of-arms which bears
      Six chevrons, gold and blue, we shall add
      A seventh: — and that shall be blood-red!

(DE GUICHE is huddled in conversation with CARBON. *Commands are given; defense-strategies planned.* CYRANO *moves to* CHRISTIAN *who, with his arms folded, has remained motionless.* CYRANO *places a comforting hand on this shoulder.* CHRISTIAN *sadly turns his head towards* CYRANO.*)*

CHRISTIAN:
      I should like to say farewell to Roxane
      In a final heartfelt letter.
CYRANO:
                              I knew you would
      So I wrote it.
CHRISTIAN:
                  You did? Let me see it.

CYRANO:
> You want to see it?

CHRISTIAN:
> > My final letter? Of course!

(Reluctantly CYRANO produces the letter and hands it to CHRISTIAN who slowly begins to scan it. Suddenly, he looks up.)

CYRANO:
> What's the matter?

CHRISTIAN:
> > Look, over here,

CYRANO:
> > What is it?

CHRISTIAN:
> This little smudge.

CYRANO:
> > Smudge?

CHRISTIAN:
> > — It's a tear.

(CYRANO takes the letter and appears to examine it closely.)

CYRANO:
> It may well be. A poet, in the throes of
> Inspiration is a victim to
> His fancy. What he loves in verse, he loves
> In fact. That's the charm of poetry.
> The letter was so moving to its subject
> It even wrung a tear from me.

CHRISTIAN:
> > You wept?

CYRANO:
> Why yes, because, my friend, to die is only
> A commonplace. Everyone lives and dies.
> But never to see her more, that's truly tragic.
> Why I would never — *(catches himself)* — we would never
> Rather *you* would never — that is —

CHRISTIAN: *(snatching the letter back)*
> > Give it here!

140

(A rumble of raised voices and a rattling coach and horse is heard in the distance.)

SENTRY: *(on the parapet)*
    Halt! Who goes there?
CARBON:
                    What is it?
SENTRY:
                        A coach sir.

(There is a burst of confusion in the camp as the CADETS scamper about to deal with some imminent danger. The following exchanges virtually overlap.)

1ST CADET:
    A coach inside the camp!
2ND CADET:
                  How can it be?
3RD CADET:
    It must have passed through enemy lines.
4TH CADET:
                          Impossible!
    Fire a warning shot!
5TH CADET:
              No, listen, listen!
6TH CADET:
    What's the driver saying?
4TH CADET:
                  Can't make it out!
3RD CADET:
    The King, the King!
2ND CADET:
              What're you saying?
6TH CADET:
                    Are you mad?
1ST CADET:
    He says he's in the service of the King.
DE GUICHE:
    Of the King!?

(The CADETS hastily fall into ranks.)

CARBON:

> Hats off — all of you!

DE GUICHE:

> Clear the way, you rabble. Make a space
> For the royal coach!

(The coach canters in. It is splattered with mud and dust. Its curtains drawn. Two lackeys behind. It lurches to a halt.)

CARBON: *(to the drummer)*

> Assembly, quick!

(The drummer begins to beat the tattoo to form ranks. The CADETS stand at attention and whip off their hats.)

DE GUICHE:

> Lower the steps!

(Two CADETS scramble to the coach to lower the steps. The door of the coach swings open.)

ROXANE: *(skipping out of the coach)*

> Good morning.

(The unexpected voice of a woman causes everyone suddenly to look up. General amazement.)

DE GUICHE:

> What? You!? — In the service of the King?

ROXANE:

> The only true king, love.

CYRANO: *(aside, breathless)*

> Merciful God!

CHRISTIAN:

> You! — But how —

ROXANE: *(blasé)*

> This war of yours was endless.

CHRISTIAN:
> But how did you —?

ROXANE: *(aside)*
> > I'll explain all later.

CYRANO: *(who has stood riveted to the spot, unable to meet her eyes)*
(aside)
> Dare I look at her?

DE GUICHE:
> > You can't stay here!

ROXANE: *(brightly)*
> Of course I can. Bring that drum up here.

(The DRUMMER rolls the drum over to her and she makes herself comfortable on it.)

> There, that's better. — You'll never believe what
> > happened.
> They fired on my coach. — Real muskets — Truly!
> It looks just like a pumpkin, doesn't it? Like in
> The fairy tale. *(throws CHRISTIAN a kiss)*
> > Good morning!
> *(looks about at all the blank faces)*
> > I must say
> No one here seems very glad to see me.
> Do you have any idea how long it takes
> To get to Arras?
> *(Noticing CYRANO)*
> > — Ah, cousin, surely
> You will greet me!

CYRANO: *(approaching)*
> > Certainly, but how —?

ROXANE:
> — Did I find you? Easy as pie. I followed
> The highways where the land was laid to waste.
> And witnessed, oh such dreadful things that I
> Could not believe my eyes. If that's the service
> Of the King, I far prefer my own.

CYRANO:
> But how did you get here?

ROXANE:

        Through the Spanish lines,
 Of course.

1ST CADET:

      You mean to say they let you through?

DE GUICHE:

 You simply galloped through the Spanish lines?

LE BRET:

 That was quite a chancey thing to do.

ROXANE:

 Now and then some hideous hidalgo
 Shoved his face inside the coach and scowled,
 But I responded with my sweetest smile;
 Whereupon the gentlemanly Spaniards,
 (Not to cast aspersions on the French),
 Like courteous cavaliers, just waived me on.

CARBON:

 A woman's smile's a very useful passport.
 But surely they would ask where you were bound.

ROXANE:

 They always did. Then I would drop my eyes
 And murmur softly: "I've a meeting with
 My lover." — Whereupon, the Spaniard with
 A look of wounded dignity would shut
 The carriage door, and with a regal gesture,
 Wave aside the muskets at my breast,
 Draw himself up to his greatest height,
 Sweeping off his pluméd hat, bow low,
 And gravely say, "Senorita, proceed!"

CHRISTIAN:

 But Roxane…

ROXANE:

      I know I said 'my lover'
 But good heavens, if I'd said "my husband,"
 I would be there still.

CHRISTIAN:

      But, but —

ROXANE:

 What *is* it?

DE GUICHE:
>> You must leave.

ROXANE:
>>>> I've just arrived!

CYRANO:
> At once!

LE BRET:
>> Even sooner.

CHRISTIAN:
>>> You must!

ROXANE:
>>>> But why?

CHRISTIAN: *(pressured)*
> Because…

CYRANO: *(pressured)*
>> In half an hour…

DE GUICHE:
>>> Or even less…

CARBON: *(tactfully)*
> It would be advisable to…

LE BRET: *(losing his cool)*
>>> Go!!!

ROXANE: *(doping it out)*
> There's going to be a battle.

ALL:
>> No!

ROXANE:
>>> I'm staying.

ALL: *(together)*
> No! — There isn't! — You can't! — Impossible!

ROXANE:
> This is my husband.
> *(Throws herself into his arms)*
>> We will die together!

CHRISTIAN:
> Your eyes are like torches!

ROXANE: *(aside to CHRISTIAN)*
>> And do you not know why?

DE GUICHE: *(exasperated)*
> We're all in mortal danger here.

ROXANE:

Danger?

CYRANO:

And indeed, it's all his doing.

ROXANE: *(turning desperately to DE GUICHE)*

Would you
Have me widowed?

DE GUICHE:

On my honor as a —

ROXANE:

I may be slightly mad — but I am staying.
It might be quite amusing.

CYRANO:

Don't tell me
You wish to play the heroine?

ROXANE:

After all,
I *am* your cousin!

1ST CADET:

We'll defend you madame,
To the death!

ROXANE: *(entering into the spirit of the occasion)*

I sensed that at once,
My loyal friends,

2ND CADET:

The whole camp smells of jasmine.

ROXANE:

What's more I've *just* the very hat for battles, here.
(she lifts a dainty hatbox out of the coach)
But then…*(looks to DE GUICHE)* perhaps the Count
Should now withdraw,
Since it may be "dangerous."

DE GUICHE: *(offended)*

You go
Too far, madame. I'm going to inspect
The arsenal and shall return. There is
Still time to change your mind.

ROXANE:

Never!

CHRISTIAN: *(pleading)*

                    Roxane!

ROXANE:

  No!

1ST CADET: *(bursting with pride)*

  She's staying here!

(The CADETS, delighted by ROXANE's fortitude begin rushing about, jostling each other, tidying themselves up.)

2ND CADET:

                 Quick, a comb!

3RD CADET:

  Some soap!

4TH CADET:

        I need some needle and thread.

5TH CADET:

                    A razor!

6TH CADET:

  Who's got a mirror?

4TH CADET:

          Oh dear, my cuffs are frayed.

ROXANE: *(to CYRANO, whose look is still urging her to go)*

  Not another word. I will not stir!

CARBON: *(having spiffed himself up, dusted himself off, polished his braid and puffed up his plume, approaches ceremoniously)*

  Since you are resolved to stay, may I

  Present the gallant men who will have

  The honor of dying in your presence.

ROXANE:

                  Please.

(Holding on to CHRISTIAN's arm, she stands formally, as if reviewing the troops, while CARBON introduces his officers.)

CARBON:

  Baron de Peyrescous de Colignac!

THE CADET: *(salutes then kisses her hand)*

  Enchanté.

CARBON:

        Baron de Casterac

  De Cahuzac —

(he salutes and kisses her hand.)
> Vidame de Malgouyré
Estressac Lesbas d'Escarabiot.
(he salutes and kisses her hand)
Chevalier d'Antignac-Juzet
(he does the same)
Baron Hillot de Blagnac-Salechan
De Castel-Crabioules —
(he does the same)

ROXANE:
> How many
Names do each of you possess?

THE BARON:
> Countless!

CARBON: *(to ROXANE)*
> And now Madame, if you'll be so kind: —
Unclench the fingers of that gentle hand
Which at present holds your handkerchief.

(ROXANE, uncertain, does so and the handkerchief flutters to the ground. At that moment, all the CADETS converge upon her to pick it up. But CARBON snatches it up first and holds it aloft.)

> My company lacked a banner. Now it has one!
The fairest standard in the camp will now
Fly proudly overhead.

ROXANE:
> It's rather small.

CARBON: *(tying it to his lance)*
> But made of lace and full of woman's fragrance.

A CADET: *(to the others)*
> Having such a vision placed before me,
I'd happily die — but if I had a little
Something in my belly —

CARBON:
> Shame, to talk
Of food when eyes can feast on such a sight.

ROXANE:
> It must be all this open air, for even
I am rather hungry. Now let me see —

Some partridges and pastry and, I think,
Some Rhenish wine. — Would someone be so kind
As to serve it up?

(The CADETS squirm with consternation.)

3RD CADET: *(aside)*
But where in hell…
ROXANE: *(overhearing)*
Why in my carriage here, of course.
ALL:
What?
ROXANE:
It's just a matter of unpacking crates
Carving up some food then serving it.
If you'll look I'm sure you'll recognize
The driver of my coach, a dear old friend.

(As they turn, RAGUENEAU removes his wide-brimmed hat and beams.)

ALL:
Ragueneau! — It's Ragueneau! — Incredible!
RAGUENEAU: *(brandishing a handful of candles)*
And all the sauces will be served up *hot!*

(There is a general acclamation as RAGUENEAU assisted by the CADETS break out the provisions.)

CYRANO: *(respectfully kissing her hand)*
Our guardian angel.
RAGUENEAU: *(standing on the coach like a Roman orator.)*
Friends — comrades,
Countrymen, and starving fellow-artists.

(The CADETS cheer him enthusiastically.)

Lend me your…teeth!

(The CADETS whoop, holler and cheer.)

The Spaniards feasted so upon our beauty,
(gesturing to ROXANE who bows coyly)
They wholly overlooked our feast!
(waves a leg of mutton)

(Cheers laughter and acclamation.)

CYRANO: *(aside to CHRISTIAN)*

                    Christian —

RAGUENEAU:
    So flattered by the chatter of the fair
    They overlooked the platter of the fowl!

(Produces a dish containing a side of ham from underneath the seat. More cheers, whoops and hollers. The dish is then eagerly passed among the troops.)

(CYRANO again tries to catch CHRISTIAN's attention.)

So besotted by the charms of Venus,
No one noticed all the trophies of
Diana, gathered from the hunt.
CYRANO:
                    I must
    Speak to you at once.
ROXANE: *(to the CADETS laden down with provisions)*
                  Spread it down
    Upon the ground.

(With the help of the FOOTMEN, a great picnic-cloth is spread on to the ground. Then, to CHRISTIAN) Lend a hand, Christian.

(CHRISTIAN goes to assist just as CYRANO was about to take him aside.)

RAGUENEAU: *(holding them aloft)*
    Peacocks and truffles.
1ST CADET: *(slicing into the ham)*
                Once, before we die
    Let's gorge ourselves —
    (catches sight of ROXANE, immediately corrects himself)

— have a snack. I mean.

RAGUENEAU: *(tossing out cushions from the coach)*
    The ortolans are mixed in with the feathers.

(There is a great uproar as the CADETS rip open the cushions.)

    Flasks of ruby — *(tossing out bottles of white wine)*
                        and flasks of topaz too.
    (tossing out bottles of red wine)
ROXANE: *(tossing a tablecloth at CYRANO)*
    Unfold this tablecloth. — Come, step lively.
RAGUENEAU: *(wrenches off one of the carriage-lamps, pries it open, potatoes
    drop out)*
    And every lamp's a tiny little larder.
CYRANO: *(to CHRISTIAN as they are both unfolding the tablecloth)*
    I've got to talk to you before you see her.
RAGUENEAU: *(more and more carried away, he produces a thin roll of sausage
    from the hollow his whip)*
    Even my whip's a secret delicacy.
ROXANE: *(filling goblets, passing out food)*
    Every man condemned is offered up
    A feast before he dies, then why not us?
    And if it's gobbled up before De Guiche,
    Returns, it's just too bad.
    (moving down the line of soldiers)
                        No need to rush.
    There's plenty of time. — Drink up, drink up.
    (pausing by a CADET)
    What's this? — Tears?
CADET: *(wiping them away)*
                        You are too good to us.
ROXANE:
    Nonsense — drink some wine. — And here's some bread
    For M'sieur de Carbon. — A knife, a plate.
    Burgundy? Or do you fancy white?
CYRANO: *(who has been following her about, helping her wait on the
    CADETS)*
    How I adore her?
ROXANE: *(to CHRISTIAN)*
                        Tell me, what will you have?

CHRISTIAN:
Nothing.
ROXANE:
You must. The muscatel's divine.
Try it with some biscuits.
CHRISTIAN: *(trying to take her aside)*
Tell me why
You've come.
ROXANE:
I will but first I've got to tend
To these poor boys.
LE BRET: *(who now returns from having carried food to the Sentinel on the rampart)*
De Guiche is coming back.
CYRANO:
Quick — hide the bottles and the baskets.
And everyone look famished as before.
(*to* RAGUENEAU)
Get back on the carriage. Everything gone!

(In an instant, the feast has vanished — disposed of in tents, hidden under cloaks, tunics and hats. Everyone again assumes a woebegone look and sits around listlessly. When DE GUICHE *is not looking, one or another takes a snap at a carrot or flips an ortolan into their mouth.)*

DE GUICHE: *(sniffing)*
There's a strong aroma in the air.

(A CADET *begins humming nonchalantly.* DE GUICHE *turns to him. He grows embarrassed.)*

What's the matter with you? Why're you blushing?
CADET:
The blood is rushing to my head because —
I know the battle's soon to come — that's all.

(Another CADET *takes up the humming very loudly.* DE GUICHE *turns to him.)*

DE GUICHE:
> What're you doing?

2ND CADET: *(tipsy)*
> > A little song — that's all.

DE GUICHE:
> You seem quite gay.

2ND CADET:
> > Always, before a battle!
> That's my style.

DE GUICHE: *(turns to CARBON to issue an order)*
> > Captain — What in heaven's —
> *(regards his smiling countenance)*
> You're looking very sunny today.

CARBON: *(hiding a bottle behind his back and quickly pulling a long face)*
> > Not I!

DE GUICHE:
> We had one cannon left. And so I've placed it
> There to fortify your men's position.

3RD CADET: *(mock-courteously)*
> How very thoughtful of you.

4TH CADET: *(in the same vein)*
> > We're quite flattered
> By your kind and courteous attention.

DE GUICHE: *(after a beat)*
> If there was anything to drink, I'd say
> You're drunk! — *(back to business)*
> > Since you're unaccustomed to
> Such guns, beware should they recoil.

1ST CADET: *(imitating the recoil of the cannon)*
> > Boom — Whissht!

DE GUICHE: *(approaches him, fuming)*
> What's got into you?

1ST CADET:
> > Gascon guns
> Do not recoil. Never! They wouldn't dare.

DE GUICHE: *(shaking him)*
> You *are* drunk!

1ST CADET: *(losing it)*
> > From the whiff of battle!
> From the taste of powder in my lungs!

DE GUICHE: *(contemptuously turns away, to* ROXANE*)*
  Have you reconsidered?
ROXANE:
                    I'm staying here.
DE GUICHE:
  There's still time to escape.
ROXANE:
                    Thank you, but no!
DE GUICHE: *(after a beat)*
  Very well then: *(to the* SENTRY*)* let me have a musket!
  (The Sentry tosses him one.)
CARBON:
  What? —
DE GUICHE:
            I too may just as well remain.
CYRANO:
  Spoken like a soldier.
1ST CADET:
                    Beneath that lace,
  It would appear there beats a Gascon heart.
DE GUICHE:
  Forsake the battlefield, when there's a woman
  In distress? — Not I, Le Comte de Guiche!

(There is a pause as all the CADETS *are forced to reassess their command-ing officer.)*

2ND CADET: *(to the* 1ST CADET*)*
  I think there's room for one more at the table.
  Wha'd you say?

(The food reappears as magically as it vanished. DE GUICHE *is mesmer-ized by the sudden sight of food, drink and feasting* CADETS*. A few sol-diers have piled a mound of food on to a plate and passed it to* DE GUICHE*. He looks at it hungrily, but strenuously falls back on his pride.)*

DE GUICHE:
  You think that I will feed on your leftovers?
CYRANO: *(saluting his beau geste)*
  You improve with every passing moment.

DE GUICHE:
I can fight the enemy exactly
As I am.

3RD CADET: *(to the 1ST CADET)*
Do you hear the accent?

1ST CADET: Gascon, through and through.

DE GUICHE:

I, an accent?

3RD CADET:
As Gasconesque as any Gascon here!

(The CADETS all look fraternally at DE GUICHE who, in spite of himself, begins to smile. A CADET hurls an apple at DE GUICHE which he promptly catches. All regard him expectantly. DE GUICHE tensely surveys his troops, the apple in his hand then, smiling again, chomps into the apple. All the CADETS explode with joy and merriment and begin a tipsy, exultant dance around the campgrounds.)

CARBON: *(having reconnoitered his way onto the parapet)*
I've placed my pikemen by the parapet.

(The tops of the pikes are now visible on the upstage end of the parapet. DE GUICHE bows to ROXANE.)

DE GUICHE: *(offering his arm)*
Shall we review the troops, madame?

ROXANE:

Let's!

(ROXANE takes DE GUICHE'S arm and head towards the parapet. As they do so, the CADETS part and doff their caps.)

CHRISTIAN: *(quickly, to CYRANO)*
What is it then? Hurry.

(As ROXANE reaches the parapet, we see the tops of the pikes lowered in a salute. This is followed by a cheer from the troops which she acknowledges with a bow.)

CHRISTIAN:

                Well, speak up.

CYRANO:

    If perchance Roxane…

CHRISTIAN:

                Well? — What?

CYRANO:

    Should speak to you about your letters —

CHRISTIAN:

                        — I know.

CYRANO:

    Don't register surprize.

CHRISTIAN:

                — About what?

CYRANO:

    I meant to mention it before but it
    Slipped my mind. The fact is —

CHRISTIAN:

                    Fact is — what?

CYRANO:

    You've written her much more than you may know.

CHRISTIAN:

    I have?

CYRANO:

        More than you may've realized.
    Since I was your voice, in a manner of speaking,
    I sometimes wrote without —

CHRISTIAN:

                  — without my knowledge?

CYRANO: *(hedging)*

    In a manner of speaking. — It was a simple matter.

CHRISTIAN:

    A simple matter? — Since we've been blockaded
    For a month, how were those letters sent?

CYRANO:

    Before daybreak, I sometimes found a way —

CHRISTIAN: *(heavily ironic)*

    Another 'simple matter' I suppose?
    How often did I write? — Two times a week? —
    Or three?

CYRANO:
                    Oftener.
CHRISTIAN:
                              Four? — Five?
CYRANO:
                                        Oftener.
CHRISTIAN:
      Every day!!?
CYRANO:
                    Sometimes twice a day!
CHRISTIAN:
      You were so obsessed with writing letters
      You risked your life — each morning??!
CYRANO: *(guiltily, seeing ROXANE return)*
                              Shh, she's coming.

(CYRANO ducks back into his tent. DE GUICHE, CARBON and the CADETS are busy in the background making preparations.)

ROXANE:
      Now Christian, finally.
CHRISTIAN:
                              Tell me, Roxane,
      I need to know. Why you journeyed over
      Ruined roads, past enemy encampments
      Just to join me here?
ROXANE:
                              Because, — your letters.
CHRISTIAN:
      My letters?
ROXANE:
                    It was they that led me on.
      Into battle — into dangers — into madness.
      Just think how much you've written in a month!
      And each one was more precious than the last.
CHRISTIAN:
      You did this — and all because of foolish
      Letters — ?
ROXANE:
                    Never call them foolish, Christian!

157

You can never know how much they meant.
I knew I loved you ever since that night
You spoke to me beneath my open window
In a voice, the likes of which I'd never
Heard before. A voice that seemed to come
Directly from your soul. And in these weeks,
In those letters, it was as if I heard
Your voice again, the way it drifted up
To me that night; — rememb'ring how you held
Me in your arms.
          And so, of course, I came;
I came at once. Who could have stayed away?
Penelope herself, so prim and proper,
At her spinning wheel, had she had
Such alluring letters from Ulysses,
Would, like frantic Helen, have tossed aside
Her loom and galloped off to Troy.

CHRISTIAN:
                      But you —

ROXANE:
I drank them up like endless stoups of wine.
Read them twice, then thrice, then read them o'er
Again. Grew faint with all the repetition.
Each page was like a petal fallen from
Your soul. The heat of all those tender phrases
Was like a fire in my grate. So keen,
So comforting, so warm…

CHRISTIAN:
                — You felt that?

ROXANE:
You know full well I did.

CHRISTIAN:
              And so, you came.

ROXANE:
Oh Christian, it's as if you were my master.
If you raised me up, still I would crumple
At your feet. Because it is my helpless
Heart that kneels before you and there's
Nothing — nothing in the world that can lift that.
(becoming contrite)

I also came, I think, to ask your pardon —
And since there is so little time that's left
I need to ask it now: I ask forgiveness —
For being young and vain and superficial,
And loving you for merely being handsome.
CHRISTIAN: *(distressed)*
    Roxane! —
ROXANE:
        'Twas crass and frivolous of me,
But now I've learned my lesson and I know
I love you deeply for yourself alone.
Love your soul more than I do your beauty
And at last, I understand them both.
CHRISTIAN:
                  But why —?
ROXANE:
It is your own true self that now I love
Not some fetching picture in my eyes.
The self that shines from deep within you.
CHRISTIAN: *(withdrawing)*
                Roxane —
ROXANE:
I know that being loved for only what
One sees — the empty vesture of a man —
Is torture to a soul as sensitive
As yours. But now your words have given you
Another frame, obliterating what
I loved before, permitting me to love
You truly as you are. My proper sight's
Restored and oh, I see now so much more.
CHRISTIAN: *(squirming)*
    But Roxane —
ROXANE:
         Can you doubt your conquest?
CHRISTIAN: *(wretched)*
    Roxane!
ROXANE:
       I realize it's hard to grasp
A love like this.

CHRISTIAN:
                    I do not want to grasp it.
I'd rather I was loved more simply for —
ROXANE:
    For what? For what any other woman
    Might, at first sight, see? — No, my love
    Is nobler than that.
CHRISTIAN:
                    I prefer it
    As it was before.
ROXANE:
                    But don't you see?
    My love is stronger now because it's found
    Your inner being. — If you had no wit —
CHRISTIAN:
    Oh, say no more.
ROXANE:
                    And even lost your looks,
    I'd love you none the less.
CHRISTIAN:
                    If I were ugly?
ROXANE:
    It wouldn't matter.
CHRISTIAN:
                    Do you mean that truly?
ROXANE:
    I'd love you still.
CHRISTIAN:
                    Unsightly and ungainly?
ROXANE:
    Yes, even then.
CHRISTIAN: *(in agony)*
            Oh God!
ROXANE: *(beaming)*
                    How good it is
    To hear your rapture.
CHRISTIAN: *(smothered by his feelings)*
                    Oghhh — oghhh.
ROXANE: *(now worried)*
                    What is it?

CHRISTIAN: *(gently extricating himself)*
    It's nothing — I need to have a moment…
ROXANE:
                             What's wrong?
CHRISTIAN: *(gesturing towards the CADETS)*
    I'm keeping you from those that have more need
    Of you; those wretched men who haven't long
    To live. — Go tend to them.
ROXANE: *(touched by his selflessness)*
                    My dear Christian.

(As she moves forward for another embrace, CHRISTIAN gently ushers her upstage where a group of CADETS gather respectfully around her.)

CYRANO: *(emerging from his tent, his armor buckled on)*
    What's wrong? You're pale as ash.
CHRISTIAN:
                  She doesn't love me.
CYRANO:
    Don't be silly, of course she does.
CHRISTIAN:
                  She doesn't!
    It's you she loves.
CYRANO:
          What?
CHRISTIAN: *(bitterly)*
            She loves my 'soul' —
    That is what she loves. And that means you!
    And you love her.
CYRANO:
          What are you saying?
CHRISTIAN: *(firmly)*
                Admit it.
    Admit it! I know it's true!
CYRANO: *(after a pause)*
             It is true.
CHRISTIAN:
    You're madly in love with her!
CYRANO: *(sadly)*
             More than that.

CHRISTIAN:
  Tell her!
CYRANO:
      What?
CHRISTIAN: *(riled)*
          Tell her that you love her!
CYRANO:
  Never!
CHRISTIAN:
      Why not?
CYRANO:
        Look at me!
CHRISTIAN:
             So what!?
  She would love me even if I were ugly.
CYRANO:
  Did she say that?
CHRISTIAN:
        She did. She said it to
  My face!
CYRANO: *(subdued)*
      I'm glad to hear that, I suppose.
  (renewing his attack)
  But listen, this is nonsense! Don't believe it!
  You cannot take a woman at her word.
  Besides, you *aren't* ugly. And what's more,
  I'd never be forgiven if you were!
CHRISTIAN:
  Let's try it and find out!
CYRANO:
        No!
CHRISTIAN: *(stroppy)*
        Let her
  Choose between us! — Tell her what you feel!
CYRANO:
  This is torture.
CHRISTIAN:
       Why should I destroy
  Your happiness just because I have
  A pretty face! — That's not fair!

CYRANO:

And I
Abolish yours because I have the gift
To put your feelings into words?

CHRISTIAN: *(insistent)*

Tell her!

CYRANO:

Don't goad me too far!

CHRISTIAN:

I'm sick to death
Of being rivals with myself!

CYRANO: *(placating)*

Christian…

CHRISTIAN:

Our secret marriage had no witnesses.
That can be annulled!

CYRANO: *(temper fraying)*

How he goes on!

CHRISTIAN:

I want her to love me as I am! —
Crude, unpolished, unpoetic me!
As I am or not at all! — I mean it!
I'm going to call her back. Let her choose!
It's you or me.

CYRANO:

It will be you.

CHRISTIAN: *(calling out painfully for her)*

Roxane!

CYRANO:

Don't, I beg you —

ROXANE: *(hurrying on, alarmed)*

What is it!

CHRISTIAN: *(looking CYRANO directly in the eye)*

Come quick.
Cyrano has important news to tell you.

(CHRISTIAN strides out as ROXANE turns to CYRANO.)

ROXANE:

What is it?

CYRANO: *(distracted, watching* CHRISTIAN *leave)*
        Oh, nothing really urgent.
You know how he exaggerates.
ROXANE:
                  I know
He doubts what I've just told him. That is very
Plain to see.
CYRANO: *(uneasily taking her hand)*
          And tell me, was it true —
What you just told him?
ROXANE:
               Of course it was.
I told him I would love him even if…
CYRANO: *(smiling sadly)*
The word is not so easy to pronounce
When I'm around —
ROXANE:
          Even if he were —
CYRANO:
I shan't be hurt. — even if he were ugly!
ROXANE:
Yes, even then.

(There is a volley of shots in the direction in which CHRISTIAN *has exited.)*

       Is that the start of battle?
CYRANO:
Unsightly?
ROXANE:
    Unsightly.
CYRANO:
       Disfigured?
ROXANE:
           Yes, even then.
CYRANO:
Grotesque?
ROXANE:
    He would never be grotesque
To me.

CYRANO:
> You'd love him still?

ROXANE:
> > I would love him

Even more.

CYRANO: *(aside)*
> > Then it's true and perhaps

There is a chance — a possibility—
(turning to her)
Roxane, hear me —

LE BRET: *(rushing in, whispering harshly)*
> > Cyrano!

CYRANO: *(turning, abruptly)*
> > > What?

LE BRET:

> > > Shhh!

(LE BRET whispers into his ear. CYRANO lets ROXANE's hand fall.)

ROXANE:
> What is it?

CYRANO: *(stunned, aside)*
> > Now, it's done.

(More shots are heard)

ROXANE:
> > > What's happening?
(She rushes up to the parapet to see for herself.)

CYRANO:
> It's done with. Now she'll never know. Never.

ROXANE: *(descending from the parapet, starts to rush off)*
> Something's happening.

CYRANO: *(holding her back)*
> > Nothing, wait.

(A group of CADETS enter trying to conceal from ROXANE what they are carrying in a blanket.)

ROXANE:
Those men…
CYRANO: *(drawing her away)*
Never mind them.
ROXANE:
What were you saying? *(distracted)*
CYRANO:
Nothing. *(gravely)*
I want you to know that of all men
Christian's mind and soul were…
(quickly correcting himself)
are of the greatest.
ROXANE:
Were? You said *were!*
(Instinctively turns to the CADETS huddled around the blanket, rushes to them with a shriek and scatters them.)
No, oh no!
CYRANO:
Finished now, all finished.

(ROXANE has uncovered the body brought in by the CADETS.)

ROXANE:
Christian, Christian.
LE BRET: *(to CYRANO, shaking his head)*
The very first shots.

(ROXANE hurls herself onto CHRISTIAN's body. The sound of gunfire is heard — first distant then close. The sound of swords and armor clanking. Drums, din and general uproar.)

ROXANE:
Christian!
CARBON: *(offstage)*
— Fall in!
ROXANE:
Christian.
CARBON: *(offstage)*
Light that fuse, and make it fast!

(RAGUENEAU, *carrying a helmet filled with water, dashes out to* ROXANE.)

CHRISTIAN: *(weakly)*

Roxane.

(ROXANE *tears a strip from her petticoat and begins dipping it in water.* CYRANO *moves in close to* CHRISTIAN *and whispers in his ear.*)

CYRANO:
I've told her all. — It's you she loves.
ROXANE: *(turning back to* CHRISTIAN*)*

My love.

CARBON: *(offstage)*
Ramrods, at the ready!
ROXANE: *(to* CYRANO*)*

He's still alive.

CARBON: *(offstage)*
Load your charges!
ROXANE: *(putting her cheek against his)*

His cheek is growing cold.

CARBON: *(offstage)*
Ready!
ROXANE: *(finding it in his bosom)*
There's a letter.
CARBON: *(offstage)*

Aim!

ROXANE: *(opening it)*

To me.

(CYRANO, *involuntarily, moves to take it up.* ROXANE *draws it away.*)

CARBON: *(offstage)*
FIRE!

(*There is a great blast of musketry followed by cries, groans and roaring sounds of battle.*)

CYRANO: *(trying to get* ROXANE *to withdraw)*
Roxane, the battle's on; the fighting's begun.

ROXANE:

    A moment longer. Now he's dead. I know.
    (wraps the blanket around the body as if to keep it warm)
    No one knew him better than you. He was
    A marvellous person, wasn't he? And a hero?

CYRANO: *(standing, with his hat in his hand)*

    He was, Roxane.

ROXANE:

                An unsung poet too.
    A fine mind.

CYRANO:

          Yes, Roxane.

ROXANE:

              A heart
    As great as was his soul. — And oh, so loving.

CYRANO: *(firmly)*

    Yes, Roxane.

ROXANE: *(throwing herself upon the body)*

             And now he's cold and dead.

CYRANO: *(aside, slowly drawing his sword)*

    And what is left for me but death as well?
    And she already mourns for me and doesn't
    Even know it.

(Trumpets sound in the distance.)

DE GUICHE: *(appears on the parapet, head bare, a wound on his forehead but with a voice of thunder)*

    That's the signal we've been waiting for.
    The troops are at the gate with reinforcements.
    Hold the line, comrades. Hold the line!

ROXANE:

    Look, tears commingled with his blood
    Upon the letter.

VOICE: *(offstage)*

             Surrender!

CADETS:

             Never! Never!

RAGUENEAU: *(having climbed inside his coach)*

    This is getting really serious.

CYRANO: *(to DE GUICHE)*
Take her away. I have to join my men!
ROXANE: *(kissing the letter)*
Blood and tears commingled…
RAGUENEAU: *(leaping from the coach to her)*
— She's fainted.
DE GUICHE: *(on the parapet, to the troops)*
Hold the line!
SPANISH VOICE: *(offstage)*
Throw down your weapons.
CADETS:
Never!
CYRANO: *(to DE GUICHE)*
Sir, you've amply proved that you're courageous!
Now prove that you are chivalrous as well.
(points to ROXANE)
Take the woman up — escape with her!
DE GUICHE: *(sweeping ROXANE up in his arms)*
All right, I will! — But try to hold the post
A little longer. I'm sure that we can win.
CYRANO: Leave that to me, m'sieur.
(calling out to ROXANE who is being sped away by DE GUICHE and RAGUENEAU)
Farewell, Roxane.

(Tumult. Cries and renewed gunfire. Wounded CADETS scramble onto the stage and fall into a heap. CYRANO, about to dash over the parapet, is intercepted by CARBON whose face and uniform are smeared with blood.)

CARBON:
Our troops are giving way. And I myself
Have twice been wounded.
CYRANO: *(shouting to the troops)*
Stand fast, my lads, stand fast!
(goes to CARBON's assistance)
There are two deaths now I must avenge.
Christian's and my own! *(to CARBON)* Courage,
Courage!
(CYRANO takes up the lance to which CARBON had tied ROXANE's kerchief. It comes to life in the wind.)

169

Flutter, little flag that bears her name.
And let the enemy beware!
(he plants it firmly in the center of the post then shouts to the CADETS)
Crush them!
Let them know the terror of our steel!
(to the fifer)
And you, let us hear the screeching of
That fife!

(The fifer, enthralled by CYRANO's spirit, plays maniacally. Wounded soldiers drag themselves to their feet. Others leap from the parapet and form a tight corps around CYRANO and his little flag. The coach is now clogged with soldiers, swords and arquebuses and resembles a makeshift fortress. From above, a soldier retreating from the action, cries: "They're climbing up the walls!" A shot rings out and he falls dead.)

Let them come. We'll welcome them
With a salute they will not soon forget!

(The Spaniards, like a horde of roaches, crawl upon the parapet with their banner raised on high. No sooner have they gained the wall then CYRANO cries out: "Fire." The CADETS volley manages to down some of the enemy, but then a voice from the Spaniard's ranks responds: "Fire!" and a deadly exchange ensues with CADETS falling to the ground on every side.)

SPANISH OFFICER:
Who are these men who scramble to their deaths
Like lovers to the beds of hungry women?
CYRANO: *(standing erect in the midst of the hail of all the bullets, declaims)*
"Behold the Sons of Gascony
Of Carbon de Castel-Jaloux."
CADETS: *(joining in with CYRANO)*
Who march to meet their destiny
A hard-fighting, hard-drinking crew…

(With this, CYRANO and his small band of survivors, mustering their last burst of energy, attack the enemy and, fighting fiercely, both sides carry their combat off stage. Beneath the broil of the battle, the sound of the poem can still be faintly heard. As the din subsides, and the lights fade, a

single spot picks out the lance on which ROXANE's *kerchief is still blowing valiantly in the wind. Upstage, another illuminates the motionless body of* CHRISTIAN.)

CURTAIN

Act V

CYRANO'S GAZETTE

Fifteen years have passed. It is now 1655. The scene: the park of the Sisters of the Cross, in Paris. Vast foliage. On the Left, a house with wide steps leading to several doors. In the center, a giant tree stands alone. Downstage and to the Right, a number of box trees, bushes and a semi-circular stone seat.

In the background, a pathway hung over with chestnut trees. Towards the Right, a door to a chapel just visible through the branches. Through the double curtain of trees, we glimpse lawns, shrubbery, rustic glades and the sky.

The small side door of the chapel opens onto a colonnade tangled with red vine which disappears on the Right as it winds past the box trees.

Autumn. The leaves are turning red. The box trees, by contrast, stand out lush and green alongside the autumnal background. Fallen leaves are strewn everywhere.

Between the seat on the Right and the single tree, a large embroidery frame, with some work started, and a small chair behind it. Baskets filled with balls of wool.

At Rise, Sisters are to-ing and fro-ing in the park; some are on the bench surrounding Mother Marguerite, an older Nun. Leaves are falling.

SISTER MARTHA: *(to MOTHER MARGUERITE)*
  Sister Claire looked in the mirror twice
  Admiring her bonnet.
MOTHER MARGUERITE: *(to SISTER CLAIRE)*
                    It's rather plain.
SISTER CLAIRE:
  And at breakfeast, Sister Martha stole
  A plum out of the tart.
MOTHER MARGUERITE: *(to SISTER MARTHA)*
                    Now that is wicked.

SISTER CLAIRE:
  It was just a tiny little glance.
SISTER MARTHA:
  It was just a tiny little plum.
MOTHER MARGUERITE: I'll mention it to M'sieur Cyrano
  When he arrives this evening.
SISTER CLAIRE:
                                  Oh no, no.
  He'd only laugh at me.
SISTER MARTHA:
                          And say that nuns
  Are all coquettes.
SISTER CLAIRE:
                    With terrible sweet tooths.
MOTHER MARGUERITE: *(smiling)*
  And therefore good.
SISTER CLAIRE:
                      But Mother Marguerite,
  Is it not a fact that Cyrano
  Has come to visit every Saturday
  For almost now ten years?
MOTHER MARGUERITE:
                                  Even longer.
  Ever since his cousin joined our Order,
  Mingling her widows weeds with our
  White linens like a raven in the midst
  Of doves.
SISTER MARTHA:
                  'Tis he alone that turns her sorrow
  Into smiles.
SISTER CLAIRE:
                  He's constantly amusing.
SISTER MARTHA:
  And always teases!
SISTER CLAIRE:
                      But in the nicest way!
SISTER MARTHA:
  I look forward to his weekly visits.
SISTER CLAIRE:
  He's such fun.

SISTER MARTHA:
>   And always eats our cookies.

MOTHER MARGUERITE:
>   But I fear, he isn't very reverent
>   And not, what one would call, a Catholic.

SISTER CLAIRE:
>   Could we not convert him, do you think?

MOTHER MARGUERITE: *(skeptically)*
>   Perhaps one day. Who knows. Greater sinners
>   Than he have sometimes found the righteous path.
>   But for the moment, do not harass him.
>   He may not come as frequently, and that
>   Would be a sin against us all.

SISTER MARTHA:
>   But God —

MOTHER MARGUERITE:
>   — Knows all about him I expect.

SISTER MARTHA:
>   He always
>   Says to me: "I ate meat last night!
>   Now what do you think of that?!" As cocky as
>   You please!

MOTHER MARGUERITE:
>   He tells you that and yet I know
>   When last he came, he hadn't tasted food
>   For several days on end.

SISTER MARTHA: *(shocked)*
>   Is that true?

MOTHER MARGUERITE:
>   He's often penniless.

SISTER MARTHA:
>   Who told you that?

MOTHER MARGUERITE:
>   M'sier Le Bret.

SISTER MARTHA:
>   Does no one offer help?

MOTHER MARGUERITE:
>   He'd not accept it. He'd be offended.

(ROXANE dressed in black mourning veils, is revealed on one of the paths

upstage. *Beside her*, DE GUICHE, *a magnificent old man, accompanies her. They move slowly.* MOTHER MARGUERITE *rises.*)

Let's in.

Madame Madeleine, appears to have
A visitor.
SISTER MARTHA: *(to SISTER CLAIRE)*
Is it the Duc de Grammont?
SISTER CLAIRE: *(looking towards DE GUICHE)*
I think it is. He's not been here for months.
SISTER MARTHA:
He's busy with the Court, the camp.
SISTER CLAIRE:

The world.

(The SISTERS exit. DE GUICHE *and* ROXANE *move downstage in silence stopping beside the embroidery frame. Pause.)*

DE GUICHE:
And here you pass your days and waste your beauty
Forever in mourning.
ROXANE: *(smiling faintly)*
Forever.
DE GUICHE:
And faithful ever?
ROXANE: *(with the same smile)*
As you say.
DE GUICHE:
At least I am forgiven.
ROXANE:
Since I've come here, yes.
(another reflective pause)
DE GUICHE:
He was a good soul.
ROXANE:
Had you known him as I…
DE GUICHE:
Alas, we weren't
Very intimate. — And his letter?
The last one? It is still next to your heart?

ROXANE: *(showing it on a velvet band around her neck)*
    Like a holy relic, it's with me still.
DE GUICHE:
    Your love for him goes far beyond the grave.
ROXANE:
    Sometimes it seems, he isn't dead at all.
    And our hearts, in some curious way,
    Are still together. Sometimes I feel his presence
    Here within these convent walls.
DE GUICHE: *(after a pause)*
                    And Cyrano?
    Do you see him often?
ROXANE:
               Every week.
    He's as punctual as a weekly journal.
    He comes and takes a seat beneath this tree.
    I sit at my embroidery and then
    I hear the stroke of four, and well I know
    Before the final stroke has tolled, I'll hear
    His cane upon the stairs. He teases me
    For my eternal needlework. And then
    Proceeds to tell me all the week's events.

(LE BRET appears on the stairs.)

    Ah, Le Bret. And tell me, how's our friend
    This week?
LE BRET:
          Not well, I fear.
DE GUICHE:
               Is he ailing?
ROXANE: *(to DE GUICHE)*
    He exaggerates.
LE BRET:
           It's as I said.
    Wretched, lonely — as I prophesied.
    Each day his letters earn him yet another
    Enemy. He rails against the nobles,
    The holy church, the hypocrites, the shams,
    The pseudo-artists and the pseudo-saints.
    None escape his vitriolic pen.
    The result? — Resentment and antagonism.

ROXANE:
> Still they fear his sword. No one dare
> Attack him there.

DE GUICHE:
> Perhaps? Who's to say.

LE BRET:
> What will finally wear him down is not
> A bludgeon or a blade, but his dismal
> Solitude. His poverty, the chill
> Of winter in his bones; the wretchedness
> Of returning to an empty room.
> All of that may down a man much faster
> Than the dagger-blow of some assassin.
> Each day he draws his belt in one notch more.
> Even his nose is like an antique piece
> Of ivory now. One thin coat, a black
> And tattered thing he wears day-in day-out.

DE GUICHE:
> Come, he's not a fading parvenu.
> He's always managed on his own and lived
> His life in his own way. No need to pity
> Such a man as that.

LE BRET:
> But my lord…

DE GUICHE:
> I know: I know. I have everything.
> He has nothing. — Still I would be proud
> To shake his hand,
> *(salutes ROXANE)*
> Now, I bid you all
> Adieu.

ROXANE:
> I'll walk with you a little way.

(The DUKE bows to LE BRET and walks with ROXANE a few steps up the stairs. Then he stops.)

DE GUICHE:
> The truth is that I envy him. Because
> When a man has everything in life,

177

Succeeds in all his goals and has nothing
To reproach himself with, still there is
A little pinch of something like remorse,
Perhaps disgust, about the life he's led.
And even as one mounts a golden staircase
In the ermine trappings of a Duke,
There trails behind a host of vain regrets;
Lost illusions of the things that were.
Just as you, dressed in your widow's weeds,
Climbing up these stairs, drag a train
Of fallen leaves behind you.

ROXANE: *(ironically)*

                     Your reverie

Does you honour.

DE GUICHE: *(suddenly turning to LE BRET)*

M'sieur Le Bret!

(to ROXANE)

                  You'll pardon me a moment.

(He goes down the stairs and speaks quietly to LE BRET.)

DE GUICHE:

It's true that no one dares attack your friend
But he is detested nevertheless.
And yesterday at Court, I heard it said
By one who'd best remain anonymous:
"This Cyrano de Bergerac is very
Prone to accidents; he best beware."

LE BRET: *(coldly)*

I thank you for the gossip.

DE GUICHE:

                       I meant it as
A friend. Keep him indoors if you can.
And urge him to be strictly on his guard.

LE BRET:

One might sooner urge the lion not
To roar. He's coming here today. I'll heed
Your words and hope that he will heed them too.

SISTER CLAIRE: *(who has hurried up the stairs to ROXANE)*

M'sieur Ragueneau would have a word.

ROXANE:

Bring him in.

(to LE BRET and DE GUICHE)
　　He's wanting consolation.
Having started as a poet, he soon
Became a singer —

LE BRET:
　　　　　　Then a bathhouse keeper.

ROXANE:
　　Beadle…

LE BRET:
　　　　　Actor…

ROXANE:
　　　　　　　Barber…

LE BRET:
　　　　　　　　　Street musician.

ROXANE:
　　What will it be today?

RAGUENEAU: *(entering on the double)*
　　　　　　Madame!

(then to LE BRET)
　　　　　　　Monsieur!

ROXANE: *(smiling)*
　　You can start to tell your troubles to
Le Bret. I'll soon be back.

RAGUENEAU:
　　But Madame —

(ROXANE exits with DE GUICHE. RAGUENEAU dashes to LE BRET and breathlessly begins.)

It's probably all for the best that she should not —
She will hear about it soon enough.
I was about to visit him — just now —
Then I saw him coming from his house
So I started off in his direction.
Then at the corner of the street — Oh God —
Was it an accident? — Who's to say? —
From the window overhead, this log,
This heavy piece of timber, falling —

LE BRET: *(shocked)*
　　　　　　Cyrano!?

179

RAGUENEAU:

    I ran to him as quickly as I could.

LE BRET:

    The scheming little cowards!

RAGUENEAU:

                             He just lay there.

    His head, this gaping hole…

LE BRET:

                             Is he dead?

RAGUENEAU:

    Yes — No! Alive — but very bloody.

    I carried him up to his room. Goodness gracious,

    Have you seen that room?

LE BRET:

                       Is he in pain?

RAGUENEAU:

    No, unconscious.

LE BRET:

                   Was a doctor called?

RAGUENEAU:

    One came out of charity, thank God.

LE BRET:

    We mustn't tell Roxane. — Not right away!

    And the doctor, what did he say?

RAGUENEAU:

                           Fever.

    Lesions of the brain — I couldn't follow.

    Complicated Roman names. If you

    Could only see him! — Great white bandages!

    There's no one there to care for him. No one!

    And if he tries to get up from his bed,

    He'll just die.

LE BRET: *(drawing him to the right)*

               We'll go by way of the chapel.

    It's faster.

ROXANE: *(appearing on the stairs, calling after* LE BRET*)*

          M'sieur Le Bret.

(They dash off without hearing her.)

Act V

They've sped away
Without a backward glance. Poor Ragueneau,
His troubles must have been unbearable.
(She comes down the stairs, moving slowly towards the tree.)
There is something beautiful about
The dying days of autumn in this place.
In spring I'm lost in hopeless melancholy
But in September, with the dregs of summer
Faintly rustling at my feet, somehow
Everything is easier to bear.
(Sits down at her embroidery frame. Two SISTERS bring a large chair from the house and place it under the tree.)
Ah, the old armchair for my friend.

SISTER MARTHA:
The finest one we have.

ROXANE:
                    Thank you, Sister.

(The NUNS exit. As she begins to embroider, the clock begins to strike four. On each strike, ROXANE closes her eyes and counts quietly to herself. On the fourth strike, she opens her eyes.)

This is the first time he's been late in, oh,
I cannot count the years. No doubt the Sister
At the gate — where's that silly thimble? —
Is delaying him with sermons on his sins.
(pause)
By now he should be totally converted.
Another leaf...
(one floats onto her embroidery frame; she brushes it off)
                Nothing would prevent him —
(finding them)
Ah, here they are, the scissors in my bag.

SISTER MARTHA: *(on the stairs)*
Monsieur de Bergerac.

ROXANE: *(not turning around)*
                    It's difficult.
To try to match up all these faded colors!

(As she embroiders, CYRANO, pale, a little shakey, his hat pulled over his

eyes, appears. SISTER MARTHA, delighted to see him, remains on the stairs. Slowly, painfully, leaning heavily on his cane, CYRANO descends the stairs. ROXANE works on obliviously then turns to CYRANO and in a tone of mock reproach begins.)

Late — tch tch tch — and for the first time
In, what is it now? Fourteen years?
CYRANO: *(hauling himself over to the chair, painfully sinks into it — his light tone in sharp contrast to his agonized expression)*
Maddening, utterly maddening.
Detained, alas, by —
ROXANE:
                By?
CYRANO:
                     A visitor,
Very unexpected.
ROXANE:
                And irritating?
CYRANO:
Untimely, I would say. Inopportune.
An old friend though, and quite familiar.
ROXANE:
Pestering you with some demand or other.
CYRANO:
Of course.
ROXANE:
             — Well, I hope you sent him packing.
CYRANO:
Temporarily, yes. "Pardon me,"
I said in my haughtiest voice, "This is
Saturday and I am otherwise
Engaged — a rendezvous I will not miss
For you or anyone, so get away!
Come back in an hour, if you like!"
ROXANE:
A rash promise cousin. I'll not let you
Go till suppertime.
CYRANO: *(gently)*
             Tonight perhaps,
I may take my leave a little sooner.

(He shuts his eyes and settles back in the chair for a moment, saying nothing. ROXANE sees SISTER MARTHA on the stairs, nods to her knowingly then turns to CYRANO.)

ROXANE: *(slyly)*
    There's someone here who's waiting to be teased.
CYRANO: *(opening his eyes suddenly)*
    Ah yes…
    (assuming a formidable, comic voice)
        Come hither, sister. — Be not afraid.

(SISTER MARTHA, anticipating the joke, approaches.)

    Ah, those pious, humble downcast eyes!
SISTER MARTHA: *(playing along, looks up and suddenly sees his face)*
    You —
CYRANO: *(indicating ROXANE)*
        Shh! — *(puts a finger to his lips)*
    (resuming the game)
        Yesterday I ate meat!
SISTER MARTHA:
    I'm sure you did.
    (aside)
        That's why he's so pale.
    (to him, quickly and in a low voice)
    Before you leave tonight stop by the pantry.
    I'll make a great big bowl of soup for you.
    If you forget now, I'll be very cross.
CYRANO: *(boisterously, in a booming voice, still playacting)*
    Ah yes!
SISTER MARTHA:
        You're quite reasonable today.
ROXANE: *(hearing them whisper)*
    Is she still converting you?
SISTER MARTHA:
                Oh never!
    God forbid.
CYRANO:
        True enough, it's only
    Struck me now. All the piety

That trickles from your lips, and yet you never
Preach or sermonize.
(fiercely, in the game again)
                    Amazing grace!
Now I'll astonish *you.*
(as if seeking a joke to top it all off, he finds one)
                    Tonight, at vespers,
I shall let you say a prayer for me!
ROXANE:
    A miracle!
CYRANO: *(laughing)*
        Sister Martha's stupefied.
SISTER MARTHA: *(softly)*
    In fact, I didn't wait for your permission.

*(She exits. CYRANO painfully making his way towards ROXANE who is
still working away at her embroidery.)*

CYRANO:
    Heavens, will I ever live to see
    The damned end of that embroidery!
ROXANE:
    Ah yes, I wondered when you'd get to that.
    (teasing)
    So predictable, my Cyrano.

(A gust of wind makes a few leaves flutter to the ground.)

CYRANO:
    Look, the leaves.
ROXANE: *(watching them in the distance)*
                    Deep Venetian red.
    Falling to the ground—
CYRANO:
                    So gracefully.
    A tiny journey from branch to earth, and yet
    Nimbly done and with a sense of style
    — A bit afraid to be compounded with
    The dust, and yet the journey's undertaken
    Without a moment's hesitation.

ROXANE:
                            Do I
    Detect a note of sadness in your voice?
CYRANO: *(recovering)*
    Not a whit, Roxane, not a whit.
ROXANE: Let's take leave of all the leaves and tell me
    All the latest news. Where's my gazette?
CYRANO:
    Ah let me see...
    (growing even paler and struggling against the pain)
                            Saturday, the nineteenth.
    The King having swallowed marmalade,
    His eighteenth portion in as many seconds,
    Caught a deadly fever and was bled.
    Marmalade was banished from the Court
    And after that, his pulse returned to normal.
    On Sunday at Her Majesty's cotillion,
    Over seven hundred candles were
    Consumed. Not eaten, only burned of course.
    They say our troops have been victorious
    In Austria. — Three witches have been hung.
    Madame d'Athis' poodle, taken ill,
    Was given half-a-dozen purgatives.
ROXANE: *(suppressing her laughter)*
    M'sieur de Bergerac, be serious!
CYRANO:
    Monday morning: — nothing special happened.
    Lygdamire took yet another lover.
ROXANE:
    Tch tch tch...
CYRANO: *(his face disfigured with the pain)*
    Tuesday, the twenty-second: The Court has gone
    To Fontainbleau. Wednesday: The Comte de Fiesque
    Called on Madame de Montglat; she said no.
    Thursday: Mancini became the Queen of France —
    Almost. Friday: Madame Montglat said yes.
    Saturday the twenty-sixth...
    (His eyes close and his head lurches forward in the seat. Silence.)
ROXANE: *(hearing nothing turns, then frightened rises)*
                            Cyrano!

CYRANO: *(slowly opening his eyes, his voice hoarse)*
What is it?
(Sees ROXANE bending over him, instinctively pulls his hat more firmly round his head, draws further back into his chair.)
It's nothing, I assure you.
ROXANE:

But —
CYRANO:
My wound from Arras — sometimes — ah well, you know —
ROXANE:
My poor friend...
CYRANO:

It's nothing. It will pass.
(forces a smile)
There, it's passed.
ROXANE: *(close beside him)*
We all have wounds, I fear.
Mine is here
(hand at her breast)
Inside this faded parchment,
Grown yellow now with age, the blood and tears
Smudged upon the page. It also smarts.

(Twilight is falling.)

CYRANO:
His letter. You said that one day I might read it.
ROXANE: *(pause)*
Would you like to — ?
CYRANO:

Yes, today I think
I would.

ROXANE: *(beat, slowly removes the little pouch from around her neck)*
Here then.
CYRANO: *(taking it)*
May I?
ROXANE:

Open it.
(ROXANE returns to her embroidery frame and resumes her work.)

CYRANO: *(unfolding it)*
>"Farewell Roxane, today I die…"

ROXANE: *(stops her work, surprised)*
>   Aloud?

CYRANO: *(reads)*
>"Perhaps tonight, my darling, my beloved.
>And O my heart is heavy with the love
>I still have not expressed and which perhaps
>You will never fully understand.
>The sight of you would oft' intoxicate
>My sense, my eyes…"

ROXANE:
>   How you read his letter.

CYRANO:
>"Drain you down to the very dregs,
>And silently would plant a kiss upon
>Each graceful little movement that you made.
>I remember most that careless little
>Gesture when you'd lightly brush the hair
>From out your eyes; the memory of that
>Now brings molten tears into my eyes…"

ROXANE: *(to herself)*
>How you read that letter — with such a —

(The night grows even darker.)

CYRANO:
>"…And makes me want to cry out in the night:
>Farewell, my own, my dearest…"

ROXANE:
>   — such a voice…

CYRANO:
>"My dearest and most precious love…"

ROXANE:
>   A voice which…

CYRANO:
>"Farewell, my love…"

ROXANE:
>   …which I have heard before. *(She approaches him softly without him noticing, passes behind the armchair, and bends over*

quietly, regarding the letter which, though held in his hand, he is not looking at. It has grown even darker now.)
CYRANO:

"I have never left you for a moment
In my thoughts, and whatever may
Occur, I shall always be beside you.
Where'ere my soul may be consigned, I know
My love for you will bridge that mortal distance.
Beyond all measure and beyond all reach…"
ROXANE: *(placing a hand on his shoulder)*

How can you read now? When it is so dark?

(He turns round and sees her close behind him, is startled for a moment then turns slowly away and lets his head fall on his chest. The twilight is now complete.)

ROXANE:

For fourteen years, you have played this role.
The loyal good old friend who comes to visit;
To be amusing.
CYRANO:

           Roxane —
ROXANE:

                It was you.
CYRANO:

No, Roxane, I swear —
ROXANE:

              I should have guessed
When I heard you speak my name.
CYRANO:

                   Not I.
ROXANE:

It was you. Now everything is clear.
The letters and the poems, that was you.
CYRANO:

No, Roxane.
ROXANE:

          The foolish words, the sighs,
The agony — it all was you.

CYRANO:
                                  I swear —
ROXANE:
    The soul that welled up from those letters, that I
    Heard that magic night — it all was you!
CYRANO:
    I never loved you —
ROXANE:
                         Yes, you loved me.
CYRANO:
                                             No.

    He loved you!
ROXANE:
                     And you love me now.
CYRANO: *(wearily)*
    No.
ROXANE:
        Now you're less convincing.
CYRANO:
                                     No,
    My best-beloved, I say I loved you not. *(CYRANO wearied and weak,
    turns directly to her and looks her directly in the eye.)*
ROXANE:
    How many things are dead; how many things
    Reborn? — Why, oh why did you keep silent
    All these many years? When you knew
    He had given nothing, and that here
    Within this letter lying on my breast,
    Your tears lay congealed.
CYRANO: *(holding out the letter)*
                              The blood was his.
ROXANE:
    And why today, do you break that silence?
CYRANO: *(looking her directly in the eye)*
    Why? Because —

    (LE BRET and RAGUENEAU come running in.)

LE BRET:
                   I knew it. Utter madness

189

Coming here!
CYRANO: *(smiling, trying to recover himself)*
        Ah, Le Bret, still scolding.
LE BRET:
    He's killed himself, madame. Leaving his bed.
ROXANE: *(something clicks inside of her as she looks from LE BRET to CYRANO)*
    Good God! — his weakness was it? — was that — ?
CYRANO:
    I didn't finish reading my Gazette.
    Saturday, the twenty-sixth: an hour or so
    Before he had a chance to eat his dinner,
    M'sieur le Bergerac sustained a blow
    Which I fear, proved fatal.
    (He removes his hat. Beneath, his head is swathed in a bandage through which the blood has clearly seeped out.)
ROXANE:
                What are you saying?
    What have they done to you?
CYRANO:
                Fate's a clown,
    You know, who loves to play his morbid jokes.
    Ambushed in the gutter, struck by a log,
    My assailant, a putrid little lackey.
    My battlefield, a common thoroughfare.
    Consistent though, up to the very end.
    I've made a mess of everything in life,
    And even now, my death.
RAGUENEAU:
               My poor m'sieur...
CYRANO: No tears, Ragueneau. That would somehow
    Make the comedy even more grotesque.
    (opens one eye and turns it on him)
    What're you up to anyway, these days?
RAGUENEAU: *(through his tears)*
    I'm a candle-snuffer now. I work
    For Molière.
CYRANO:
           Molière, I am impressed.

RAGUENEAU:
    But tomorrow night I will resign.
    Yesterday they played 'Scapin' and lo,
    There's one whole scene he stole direct from you!
LE BRET:
    Word for word! I've seen it too!
RAGUENEAU:
                                The one
    That starts: "Now what the devil's he doing here."
CYRANO:
    It got its laughs, I hope.
RAGUENEAU: *(sobbing)*
                        Oh sir, they laughed
    And laughed and laughed.
CYRANO:
                        That seems to be my fate —
    To furnish lines for others, then be forgot.
    (to ROXANE)
    Remember when our Christian stood beneath
    Your balcony and poured his aching heart out
    Underneath the stars, and then climbed up
    To claim the precious prize while I, like some
    Pathetic prompter hid myself in darkness?
    Well, there you have a little microcosm
    Of my entire life. A bitter kind
    Of justice does prevail. Molière has genius,
    Christian, he had beauty.

(The chapel bell begins to sound. Above the stairway, the NUNS in a formal procession shuffle to their prayers.)

                        They're off to prayer.
    The evening bell invites them.
ROXANE: *(calling to them)*
                        Sister— Sister — !
CYRANO: *(taking her hand)*
    Don't leave! — I may be gone when you get back.

(The NUNS are now in the chapel and the sound of the organ emanates softly from within.)

Ha, exactly what I need just now:
Some harmony in my life. *(of the organ)* Do you hear?
ROXANE:
You shall not die. I won't permit it. I love you.
CYRANO:
No, you've got it wrong, my dear. Don't you
Recall when Beauty said: 'I love you' to
The Beast, his ugliness transformed and lo,
A fairy prince was standing in his place.
But as you see, — I am just the same.
ROXANE:
I have brought this misery upon you,
I alone. The fault is mine.
CYRANO:
      No no,
On the contrary, I'd never have known
The splendors of woman, the utter sweetness of
Femininity, if not for you.
My mother never deigned to look at me.
I had no sister, and later came to dread
The mocking eye of one who might pretend
To be a sweetheart. But all because of you,
I've had th'abiding joy of one dear friend;
Both the pleasure and the pangs, of a
Woman in my life.
LE BRET: *(pointing to the moon which is now visible behind the trees)*
      Your other good old friend
Has also come to see you.
CYRANO: *(smiling at the moon)*
      So I see.
ROXANE: *(to herself)*
I never loved but one man in my life,
How cruel of God to make me lose him twice.
CYRANO:
I'll soon be up there in the moon, Le Bret
And ironically, without the aid of
Any flying machine.
ROXANE:
      What are you saying?

CYRANO:

'Twould be a fitting paradise for me.
I'm sure I'd find some others of my ilk —
Plato, Socrates and Galileo.

LE BRET: *(rebelling)*

No, no! — This is stupid and unjust!
Such a poet — such a friend — to die —
It cannot, must not, shall not be!

CYRANO: *(hand to head)*

That sound

Again. Le Bret, scolding.

(LE BRET unable to sustain his emotions, breaks down. CYRANO tries to raise himself in the chair, his stare is glassy and unfocused.)

"Behold the Sons of Gascony
Of Carbon de Castel-Jaloux.
Who march to meet their destiny... their destiny..."
—The elementary mass —ah, there's the point.
Ergo... It must follow —

LE BRET: *(quietly to the others)*

He's delirious.

CYRANO:

As Copernicus pointed out...or was it Kepler?
(more and more delirious)
"What in hell was he up to there?
What in hell was he doing there?"...
(he declaims, rhetorically)
Philosopher, scientist,
Poet, swordsman, musician,
Space Traveller Extraordinaire
And lover too, (what little good it did him.)
Here lies Hercule-Savinien
De Cyrano de Bergerac
He tried all things,
And all things did lack.
(suddenly light and casual)
Well, pardon I crave, it is well past seven.
My moonbeam is here to take me to heaven.
(He slumps backward into the chair, almost unconscious. The sound of

ROXANE'*s sobbing brings him round. Gradually, his sense is restored.*
Gently, he caresses her veil.)
I would not have you shed one tear the less
For Christian, brave and true. And when my weary
Bones are stored beneath the earth and you,
In widows' weeds, are crouched beside the grave,
Let your mourning prayers embrace us both.

ROXANE:
I swear it.

CYRANO: *(Suddenly, feverously, he raises himself in the chair and pushes her*
away.)
Not here. Not like this. Not sitting down!

(They rush towards him; he motions them away.)

Let no one help me. — None I say!
(He supports his back against the tree trunk. There is a pause.)
It's coming — I feel myself — encased in marble,
Boxed in lead. — The gravel in my mouth!
Let him come. He'll find me on my feet!
(draws his sword)
The blade clutched in my hand!

LE BRET:

                    Cyrano!

(ROXANE reels, is close to fainting.)

CYRANO:
I see him grinning, that grisly little grin,
He's peering at my nose. *(sneeringly)* "Take a
                       good look!"
'Useless?' you say — perhaps! — but a man doesn't always
Fight to win. 'Tis *best* when all's in vain!
And now they all surround me; a hundred to one.
I know you all, my ancient adversaries;
(lunges at them as he speaks)
Falsehood !
(lunge)
Prejudice !
(lunges)

Compromise!
(lunges)
Cowardice!
I, surrender? Make terms? Never! Never!
Old Vanity, you too! I knew you'd get me
In the end. — No matter, I fight on,
And on, and on, and on, and on and on!
(He swings his sword in great circles on every side, breathlessly gasps for
air then speaks with a calm resolve.)
All my laurels you have stripped away
And all my roses too, yet one thing still
Remains, my own unto the very end.
And when tonight I stand at heaven's gate
And sweep away the stars from that blue threshold,
It will, despite you all, remain unsullied
And unspoiled. — And that's…
(The sword falls from his hand, he slumps into LE BRET's *arms.* ROXANE
bends close to his face to make out his words. CYRANO *opens his eyes,*
looks into her eyes and says with a faint smile)
　　　　　　　　　　　　　…my soldier's plume.

CURTAIN

Smith and Kraus *Books For Actors*

MONOLOGUE SERIES

The Best Men's / Women's Stage Monologues of 1993
The Best Men's / Women's Stage Monologues of 1992
The Best Men's / Women's Stage Monologues of 1991
The Best Men's / Women's Stage Monologues of 1990
One Hundred Men's / Women's Stage Monologues from the 1980's
2 Minutes and Under: Character Monologues for Actors
Street Talk: Character Monologues for Actors
Uptown: Character Monologues for Actors
Monologues from Contemporary Literature: Volume I
Monologues from Classic Plays

FESTIVAL MONOLOGUE SERIES

The Great Monologues from the Humana Festival
The Great Monologues from the EST Marathon
The Great Monologues from the Mark Taper Forum
The Great Monologues from the Women's Project

YOUNG ACTORS SERIES

Great Scenes for Young Actors from the Stage
Great Monologues for Young Actors
Multicultural Monologues for Young Actors
Multicultural Scenes for Young Actors
Villeggiature: The Trilogy Condensed, Goldoni, tr. by Robert Cornthwaite

SCENE STUDY SERIES

Scenes From Classic Plays 468 B.C. to 1960 A.D.
The Best Stage Scenes of 1993
The Best Stage Scenes of 1992
The Best Stage Scenes for Women from the 1980's
The Best Stage Scenes for Men from the 1980's

CONTEMPORARY PLAYWRIGHTS

Romulus Linney: 17 Short Plays
Eric Overmyer: Collected Plays
Lanford Wilson: 21 Short Plays
William Mastrosimone: Collected Plays
Horton Foote: 4 New Plays
Terrence McNally: 15 Short Plays
Women Playwrights: The Best Plays of 1992
Women Playwrights: The Best Plays of 1993
Humana Festival '93: The Complete Plays
Humana Festival '94: The Complete Plays

GREAT TRANSLATION FOR ACTORS SERIES

The Wood Demon: Anton Chekhov *translated by N. Saunders & F. Dwyer*
The Seagull: Anton Chekhov *translated by N. Saunders & F. Dwyer*
Three Sisters: Anton Chekhov *translated by Lanford Wilson*
Mercadet: Honoré de Balzac *translated by Robert Cornthwaite*
Villeggiatura: A Trilogy by Carlo Goldoni *translated by Robert Cornthwaite*

CAREER DEVELOPMENT BOOKS

The Actor's Chekhov
Kiss and Tell: Restoration Scenes, Monologues, & History
Cold Readings: Some Do's and Don'ts for Actors at Auditions
A Shakespearean Actor Prepares
Auditioning For Musical Theater
The Camera Smart Actor

If you require pre-publication information about upcoming Smith and Kraus books, you may receive our semi-annual catalogue, free of charge, by sending your name and address to *Smith and Kraus Catalogue, P.O. Box 127 One Main Street, Lyme, NH 03768 phone 1-800-895-4331, fax 1-603-795-4427.*